DEMOCRACY, POWER, AND INTERVENTION

in Latin American Political Life:

A Study of Scholarly Images

by
KENNETH F. JOHNSON/ MILES W. WILLIAMS

SPECIAL STUDIES No. 17

center for latin american studies
arizona state university, tempe, arizona 85281

LIBRARY OF CONGRESS CATALOGING IN PUBLICATION DATA

Johnson, Kenneth F
  Democracy, power, and intervention in Latin American political life.

    (Special study - Center for Latin American Studies, Arizona State University ; 17)
     1. Latin America--Politics and government--1948- 2. Democracy. 3. Economic assistance, American--Latin America. I. Williams, Miles, joint author.
II. Title. III. Series: Arizona. State University, Tempe. Center for Latin American Studies. Special study - Arizona State University, Center for Latin American Studies ; 17.
F1414.2.J63   320.9'8'03   78-10689
ISBN 0-87918-044-7

Copyright © 1978--Arizona Board of Regents
Arizona State University
Center for Latin American Studies
Tempe, Arizona 85281

All rights reserved. No part of this publication may be reproduced or transmitted in any form or by any means, electronic or mechanical, including photocopy, recording, or any information storage or retrieval system, without permission in writing from the publisher.

PREFACE AND ACKNOWLEDGMENTS

This publication brings to partial fruition an ambitious research endeavor which Russell H. Fitzgibbon started in 1945. We offer this as reputational research, an effort to quantify the subjective, but informed, reflections of scholars in the field of Latin American politics, and we are aware of the limitations inherent in this procedure. Certain critics of the method are cited herein as are a number of our own efforts to purge the study of some of its "methodological impurities." Essentially, we try to show trends in the reputational "weathervane" of Latin American political democracy as reflected by selected panels of North American experts. We are not unaware of the dangers of ethnocentric bias that may be lurking within the shadow of our approach and methods.

A large measure of thanks goes to Merle Kling and James Wilkie who have given advice and encouragement over recent years. Edward J. Williams, Marvin Alisky, Stephen Mumme, and Larry Koslow have given valued advice for which we are grateful. John D. Martz criticized an earlier version of the manuscript and we are especially grateful to him. Jerry Ladman, Dave Foster, Mary Holguin, and the Center staff at ASU have been excellent colleagues to work with and their suggestions are much appreciated. Thanks are due Lee Pappas for editing and Lynnette Winkelman for typing the final manuscript. Most important of all, however, are the many colleagues (the majority from either political science or history) who took the time to answer our questionnaire. Thanks to them we are able to offer here a new dimension to the Fitzgibbon-Johnson Image Index, a measurement we have chosen to call the PRC or power rating coefficient. This is balanced with a normative and humanistically anchored construct which we chose to call the "Macondo Syndrome." The reader will decide if our attempted "marriage" between statistics and heart-felt instinct makes any sense.

My partner Miles Williams is currently in Bogotá trying to refine both our normative and quantitative analytic techniques, and to him goes a rather special vote of thanks for helping to engineer a bridge between the social sciences and the humanities, one which we hope to test further in 1980.

Kenneth F. Johnson
Saint Louis,
Summer 1978

TABLE OF CONTENTS

CHAPTER		PAGE
ONE	DEMOCRACY IN LATIN AMERICA: NORMATIVE AND HUMANISTIC DIMENSIONS	1
TWO	DEMOCRACY, POWER, AND THE MACONDO SYNDROME	7
	VIGNETTES AND REALITY	7
	NORMATIVE THEORETIC DIMENSIONS	10
THREE	MEASURING THE SCHOLARLY IMAGE DEMOCRACY IN LATIN AMERICA	22
	THEORETICAL AND METHODOLOGICAL UNDERPINNINGS	22
	THE CHANGING SCHOLARLY IMAGE OF DEMOCRACY IN LATIN AMERICA	24
	POLITICAL DEMOCRACY: FOUR CASES	32
	SUMMARY AND CONCLUSION	32
FOUR	THE POLITICAL DEMOCRACY-POLITICAL POWER NEXUS	37
	INTRODUCTION	37
	THE POWER RATING COEFFICIENT	38
	SUMMARY	46
FIVE	POWER, DEMOCRACY AND DEPENDENCY THE HEMISPHERIC PICTURE OF INTERVENTION	48
	ANTECEDENTS	50
	THE ALPRO SYNDROME	52
	THE IMPACT OF U.S. AID ON LATIN AMERICAN DEMOCRACY	54
	SUMMARY AND CONCLUSIONS	60
SIX	CONCLUSIONS	64

LIST OF TABLES AND FIGURES

TABLE		PAGE
1	DEMOCRATIC RATING COEFFICIENT (DRC) FOR SEVEN FITZGIBBON-JOHNSON IMAGE INDEX STUDIES (1945-1975)	27
2	RATING COEFFICIENTS OF 15 ITEMS FOR ALL COUNTRIES USED IN FITZGIBBON-JOHNSON IMAGE INDEX EXPERIMENTS (1945-1975)	28
3	THE CHANGING SCHOLARLY IMAGE OF DEMOCRACY IN LATIN AMERICA (1945-1975)	29
4	POWER RATING COEFFICIENTS (PRC) OF SELECTED POLITICAL ACTORS IN LATIN AMERICA (1975)	39
5	THE INTERRELATIONSHIP BETWEEN THE POWER OF POLITICAL CONTENDERS IN LATIN AMERICA	41
6	POWER, DEMOCRACY, AND STABILITY IN LATIN AMERICA	45
7	UNITED STATES ECONOMIC AND MILITARY ASSISTANCE TO LATIN AMERICA (1962-1974)	56
8	PER CAPITA UNITED STATES MILITARY AND ECONOMIC ASSISTANCE TO LATIN AMERICA (1962-1974)	57
9	THE RELATIONSHIP BETWEEN POWER, DEMOCRACY AND U.S. ASSISTANCE TO LATIN AMERICA	58

FIGURE		
1	SUBSTANTIVE CRITERIA OF THE FITZGIBBON-JOHNSON IMAGE INDEX	25
2	THE SOCIAL AND ECONOMIC CORRELATES OF POLITICAL DEMOCRACY AND SYSTEM STABILITY	31
3	COMPARATIVE DEMOCRATIC RATING COEFFICIENTS: FOUR CASES	33

CHAPTER ONE

DEMOCRACY IN LATIN AMERICA:
NORMATIVE AND HUMANISTIC DIMENSIONS

Recurring cycles of conflict arising from incompatible value requirements typify much of the political life of Latin America. In the ongoing struggle between "elitists" and "populists" the quest for social and political democracy has often been detoured. Not unexpectedly, fears of what "mass man" might do to himself and others if allowed to exercise "pure" democracy have issued forth from the pens of many writers in the Hispanic tradition. Ortega y Gasset may have offered the prototypal expression of this sentiment. In Spanish America other great thinkers refined the theme. One of Argentina's most perceptive minds, Eduardo Mallea, saw the anachronism of "elitist democracy" in conflict with "mass democracy," a struggle whose likely outcome would be destruction of the ideal type (if such ever existed anywhere except in the mind of Mallea). He believed that Argentina's great destiny lay in a "spiritual architecture" via which the true and hidden nature of man's being is released.[1] Mallea glorified Argentina's rural countrymen as the genuine human element of his country whose integrity could lead to greatness, but unfortunately Argentina in the early twentieth century was governed by city men whose nature had been distorted into the practice of social fraud presided over by politicians who substituted a "representation" of life for really living.[2] As a consequence Mallea saw life in Argentina as muted, the streets swallowed in darkness, the faces and minds of the people immersed in a great internal marshland.[3] Out of this gloom emerged the singular feature that would typify the political life of his country well into the 1970s, what Malea termed *los gobernadores de las tinieblas*, governors of darkness![4]

Such pessimism is not a unique commentary on the political life of most of Latin America today and it is relevant to a theoretic and statistical effort to conceptualize and reflect (if not to measure) the thrusts and consequences of the conduct of political democracy. Few Latin American states or their peoples profess antidemocracy as a national goal; almost all claim to have, or to be working toward, political democracy in one form or another. But there remains the dilemma of reconciling "mass democracy" with its potential for stamping out individuality, and "elite guided democracy" with its potential for abridgment of human liberties.

Individuality, it is urged, is the core idea in democratic theory and it is feared that "mass culture" values will stultify the uniqueness of the human spirit.[5] In contrast others have argued that democracy as practiced contemporaneously is a "pious fraud" and that its real human benefits could be secured by scientifically ascertaining the true desires of the population and pursuing their fulfillment via a science of "cultural engineering," this presided over by a set of self-identified planners and managers. Admittedly, such would be a limited form of Fascism but not necessarily inconsistent with the professed

1

goals of democracy.[6] Elite theorists have eschewed preoccupation with the structure of the democratic process and stressed its real life impact as reflected in human satisfactions and happiness. Importantly many such "democratic elitists" believe that the vast majority of people want to have their lives managed benevolently, given regular consultation and managerial accountability.

Such normative elitism has typified much of the political thinking of Latin America. For instance, the Somoza dynasty in Nicaragua (that has ruled under one guise or another since the late 1930s) ennobles itself with democratic trappings such as elections and puppet two-party parliaments. Spokesmen for that regime say the dynasty is benevolent and is best qualified to interpret the best interests of the people. But contemporary scholarship has shown Nicaragua to be a brazen dictatorship where human rights are violated, torture and assassination are standard political tools, resulting in a social and political atmosphere that has generated one of the world's highest rates of suicide and alcoholism. In Nicaragua today democracy is nowhere in sight.[7]

Literary minds have probed the depths of the political psyche in other countries. The distinguished contemporary Argentine novelist Julio Cortázar has observed the innate emotional need of his countrymen for a political *status quo* that is dominated by elites, *caudillos*, soothsayers, messiahs, whose magic watchwords come to be expressed as "isms."[8] Stated succinctly, this thesis is that the people have an innate spiritual need to seek refuge in "thaumaturgical words," miracle-working amulets that will give them a comforting (albeit false) sense of political cohesion and identity. They need a symbolic presence that continually inspires group attachment, patriotic spirit, and loyalty. To be useful the symbols, words, leaders, or "isms" must be such that their emotive qualities may at least be feigned.[9] Destroy this symbolic presence by sullying the "thaumaturgical words" of "isms" and the unifying fabric of the polity atrophies with resultant instability and violence. This is the reality of what we may more appropriately term the "undemocracy" prevailing throughout much of Latin American political life today.

Some Latin American scholars have also lamented the lost opportunity to capitalize on a past which seemed to portend the good political life as they saw it. Mexico's philosopher-poet Octavio Paz writes that New Spain from the second half of the sixteenth century to the end of the eighteenth century was a stable, peaceful, and prosperous society, this under the tutelage of a series of viceroys. New Spain frequently knew what Paz terms "good government."[10] Not that all viceroys were good and benevolent governors; but there was a sufficient division and balancing of powers among the state, the Church, and the *audiencia* so that the masses were consulted indirectly and exercised influence under a sort of guided democracy. At least the colonial government was forced to seek a measure of public consensus. But populist revolutionaries and misguided adventurers later destroyed this fertile democratic potential. Paz writes, "In this sense, the system of New Spain was more flexible than the present presidential regime [of Mexico in the 1970s]. Under the mask of democracy, our presidents are constitutional dictators in the Roman style. The only difference is that the Roman dictatorship lasted six months, while ours lasts six years."[11]

We believe intuitively, and think we know empirically, that ideal types ("pure democracy") do not exist in the phenomenal world. Efforts to define democracy with an eye to operationalizing concepts in a real life setting are inevitably accompanied by caveats lending flexibility that may cover unforeseen circumstances. Thus, in a widely lauded text, the political theorist Lyman T. Sargent contends that the most significant elements in a democratic political system would be some degree of citizen involvement in political decision-making, a measure of equality among citizens, guarantees for key political liberties, a system of representation, and an electoral system involving majority rule.[12] Sargent must leave his formulation general for he cannot pretend to specify what democratic variations will be most appropriate, and in what intensity, for all societies.

A political sociologist, S. M. Lipset, tries to be somewhat more precise. Democracy in his framework is defined as "a political system which supplies regular constitutional opportunities for changing the governing officials."[13] He also specifies three basic conditions for democracy, a belief system that legitimizes the political system and allows the operation of free press, political parties, etc., a set of political leaders in office and elected popularly, and alternative sets of potential political leaders out of office who criticize the incumbents and make them accountable *vis-à-vis* the loyal opposition and its public. This constitutes an ideal type that has been labeled "shared democracy."

Other theorists like the political psychologist Christian Bay have treated democracy as a catalyst for individual freedoms and in the context of mental health. In stating his concept of potential freedom, Bay focuses on the degree to which value systems may have become institutionalized impediments.[14] He argues, "For the potential freedom of the individual, the difference between high and low degrees of institutionalization is more important than the difference between democracy and dictatorship. Individual autonomy is severely limited in a strongly tradition-bound society, whether the limited sphere of political authority is or is not exercised from a democratic basis."[15] He admits however that the exercise of power and authority is likely to be more ruthless in a nondemocratic country because there criticism of the regime more easily gets branded as subversive. Many of Bay's strictures on democracy are similar to those of the writers cited above. He offers freedom from coercion as the supreme good, presumably achieved more readily in democratic than in nondemocratic societies, and freedom of speech as the collateral second priority.[16]

All of the foregoing portends the necessity for a major cross-disciplinary approach to realistic and systematic study of political democracy. In the pages to follow we will draw on insights from both literary and social science scholars. These schools, or approaches, are viewed herein as complementary rather than mutually exclusive or antagonistic. We believe that literary glimpses of the political process may elucidate quantitatively expressed data of an evaluative, reputational, or "soft" nature. We are interested in the degree, for example, to which literary scholars (whose culturally rooted works we accept as valid evidence) may confirm the dictates of Bay on the effects of tradition, those of Lipset on the criterion of power sharing, or of Sargent on equality. We will be concerned with how social science data can reflect upon the way the political system may have generated distortions in individual personalities, as in Mallea's words, or how the psychic requirements of individuals may, in fact, have shaped the system as in that of Cortázar. And if there is any way to relate our data to the contention of Paz that democracy is a "mask," or to that of Skinner that it is a "pious fraud," then we will do so. Our data base was not constructed with a preconceived plan to touch on all these points, yet the various sources of insight may complement each other. That form of symbiosis is a major goal of this undertaking.

Additionally it is our intention to reflect upon the democratic (or undemocratic) impact of foreign interventionism, specifically United States foreign assistance, on the political systems of Latin America. Admittedly we may be able to show statistical correlations at a high level of significance within probability theory, but this is not causal proof. Causal relationships must be inferred and bolstered with our supplementary evidence. And here again there is room for reinforcing our judgments with the insights of literary scholars. Witness: the matter of foreign assistance, a type of interventionism. Graham Greene stated the case forcefully: "Malnutrition is much safer for the rich than starvation. Starvation makes a man desperate. Malnutrition makes him too tired to raise a fist. The Americans understand that well. The aid they give us makes just that amount of difference. Our people do not starve. They wilt."[17]

Because of the prevalence of extralegality (subversion of constitutionalism) as a political skill in the Latin American tradition we cannot expect performance throughout the hemisphere to conform to or even approach an ideal type, not even to the extent that the United States or Canada might be imperfect reflections of that very ideal. Put succinctly we must conceptualize democracy with sufficient flexibility so as not to brand all twenty of Latin America's principal nations as dictatorships just because their governments achieved power via coups and other non-democratic means. In the final analysis we will distinguish between political democracy and social democracy as a way of obviating some of the dilemma of operationalizing democratic theory amid the chaos of Latin American politics. We will postulate, as Leslie Lipson put it, "If one or two elections do not create a democracy, neither do one or two *coups d'état* confirm the opposite. What should always be remembered is that every people has to win its own democracy for itself."[18]

For purposes of the present analysis we understand that a strongly democratic political system would have all of the following characteristics to some degree:

1. Popular sovereignty exercised through competing interest groups that vie for power and leadership within a fixed and impartial set of rules that are applied equally to all participants.

2. The state and its personnel exist to serve the public, not to rob it, and there is a recognized norm distinguishing between that which is public and that which is private.

3. Some free and honest procedure for selecting leaders of the state that will be competitive, popular, and offer a substantive ideological choice among candidates and issues.

4. Leadership elements so chosen will be perpetually (or periodically) subject to public review, challenge, and/or removal from office, again under an impartial and equitably applied set of rules.

5. The stakes in the power struggle (which is politics) will not be so high as to make it impossible for one politically relevant group to accept an adverse popular judgment *vis-à-vis* its preferred candidate or policy.

6. The overall thrust of the political system is conducive to individual self-realization (as opposed to fascism in which the individual is sacrificed to the alleged organic unity of the nation-state or communism in which the individual is subordinated to the class struggle).[19]

A glance over the hemisphere in the 1970s will show that, in substance, not many Latin American states meet all of these criteria. Even when applied to North America, democracy becomes a culture-relative concept. The best we can do is locate the Latin American nations along a continuum, allowing their own cultural norms to set standards for excellence and avoiding any direct comparison for the moment with the United States or Canada. We will therefore begin with a culturally well rooted model drawn from the pen of one native Latin American scholar and embellish it into a broad reflection of some of the more salient dilemmas involved in the quest (if indeed there is one) for political democracy in Latin America.

FOOTNOTES: CHAPTER ONE

1. Eduardo Mallea, *Historia de una pasión argentina* (Buenos Aires: Sur, 1937), p. 248.
2. Mallea, p. 65.
3. Mallea, p. 200.
4. Mallea, p. 301.
5. David E. Ingersoll, *Communism, Fascism, and Democracy* (Columbus: Charles E. Merrill, 1971), p. 174.
6. B. F. Skinner, *Walden Two (revisited)* (1948: reprinted New York: Macmillan, 1976), pp. 248-264.
7. See Richard Millett, *Guardians of the Dynasty* (Maryknoll: Orbis, 1977).
8. Julio Cortázar, *Libro de Manuel* (Buenos Aires: Editorial Sudamericana, 1973), pp. 261-262.
9. A good example of such symbol propagation is Juan Domingo Perón's Red Book, *El libro rojo de Perón* (Buenos Aires: A. Peno Lillo Ed., 1973).
10. From Octavio Paz's introduction to Jacques Lafaye, *Quetzalcóatl and Guadalupe: The Formation of Mexican National Consciousness 1531-1813* (Chicago: University of Chicago Press, 1976), p. xviii.
11. Paz, *Quetzalcóatl*. . . .
12. Lyman T. Sargent, *Contemporary Political Ideologies*, 3rd ed. (Homewood, Illinois: Dorsey Press, 1975).
13. From Seymour M. Lipset, "Some Social Requisits of Democracy," in Roy Macridis and Bernard Brown, eds., *Comparative Politics: Notes and Readings*, 5th ed. (Homewood: Dorsey Press, 1961), p. 115.
14. Bay understands potential freedom largely as the ability, unhampered by external force, to become what one's innate talents and desires dictate. From his *The Structure of Freedom* (New York: Atheneum, 1965).
15. Bay, p. 317.
16. Bay, p. 374.
17. From his *The Honorary Consul* (New York: Pocket Books, 1974), p. 128.
18. From his *The Democratic Civilization* (New York: Oxford, 1964), p. 589.
19. As set forth originally in Kenneth F. Johnson, "Scholarly Images of Latin America Political Democracy in 1975," *Latin American Research Review* 11, 2 (Summer 1976), 129-41.

CHAPTER TWO

DEMOCRACY, POWER, AND THE MACONDO SYNDROME

VIGNETTES AND REALITY

Dictators, whether would-be or actual, demand popular adulation. If it is not forthcoming spontaneously (as in Perón's Argentina) the adulation can be fabricated. Thus Colombia's ex-dictator Gustavo Rojas Pinilla once convoked a special celebration to honor himself. On one evening during November, 1967, in Bogotá's luxurious Hotel Tequendama a group of his faithful gathered to hear the aging tyrant compared favorably with one of the characters in the novel *One Hundred Years of Solitude* by Gabriel García Márquez. The reference was to the mythical community of Macondo and a specific character in the novel, Aureliano Buendía, who refused to shirk his country's challenge; hence he merited adulation.

Like Rojas Pinilla during his period of office (1953-57) Colonel Aureliano Buendía was popularly admired for his fabricated mystique of greatness (a pretended near thaumaturgical quality), he was personally vain, lacking a well-defined political ideology, and his family lived (in the novel) under the constant fear of a gypsy prophesy that one of their offspring would be born with the tail of a pig. That event would eventually usher in the destruction of the utopian community of Macondo. The chief protagonist (Buendía) ultimately dies innocuously along with the village. That also happened to Rojas Pinilla in real life in 1973 and his political movement, like Macondo, began to atrophy. Rojas Pinilla's populistic visions (he wanted to be another Perón) were exploded by conflict within the real world, just as the literary vision of Macondo was reduced to debris by a flood via the novelist's pen. Macondo can be said to constitute something of a behavioral model for much of Latin American political life in the 1970s. Here is our resumé of what we think Macondo was and is, albeit with certain conceptual liberties that García Márquez might not fully approve.

Everyone who lives in Macondo seems to have had his destiny fixed at birth. Macondo is creation and recreation in a single instant. It is the simultaneousness of what *has* happened, combined with what *is* happening, added to that which *will* come to pass, all in mixed time cycles. The primitive inhabitants of Macondo have a measure of ingenuity. They create certain dilemmas of want satisfaction through basic technological discoveries which aid them in feeding themselves more efficiently. But the more complex their society becomes the greater their need for government (or the more inevitable the evolution of some part of their social organism into a government). Their socioeconomic development brings government from without.

Thus the people of Macondo discover gradually that they live in a country called Colombia and its government, an external force, has an interest in regulating their lives. To this is added a more distant and ominous foreign influence, a North American banana company that comes to exploit both the people and their lands. The company and the government conspire to rule Macondo. The community begins to change from a patriarchal society into one with formal social controls via use of police power. The banana company brings the profit motive to Macondo which begins to erode the family structure that once governed the society; along with this comes the formation of labor unions.

Through the intricate web of story-telling which makes the job of extracting political theory difficult, this novel is a melancholy summing-up. The people are not governed benevolently, they are pariahs. The government lies, cheats, tortures, and ennobles itself with the artificial division of the political spectrum into Liberals (who are liberal only with benefits for themselves) and Conservatives (who devote their time not to conserving but to conspicuous consumption and to destruction). This led Colonel Aureliano Buendía to remark that "the only difference between Liberals and Conservatives [in Colombia, but symbolically elsewhere in Latin America] is that the former go to mass at five and the latter go at eight."

As the society becomes interdependent with the outside world a government overseer called a *corregidor* arrives. He is told by the elders of Macondo that "we don't need a *corregidor* [literally a corrector] because there is nothing to correct" but the forces from without see it differently. A blood tie develops between the people and the authority when Aureliano marries the daughter of Apolinar Moscote, the *corregidor*. This helps the latter to consolidate his power and authority somewhat, but at the same time it becomes necessary for armed policemen to come to the village for the first time. Power has become armed force. Supposedly Macondo is modernizing for now there is a defined order of authority that must be maintained under the threat of physical coercion. The people are then told about the political abyss between Liberals (who favor giving rights to illegitimate children and granting regional autonomies) and Conservatives (who claim to have a direct mandate from God and Jesus to keep the county morally pure and governed from the center). The potential for converting power into violence, hence into terror, has become more real.

Corruption, a traditional Latin American value dilemma, is present in Macondo. Aureliano witnesses his first electoral fraud; his own father-in-law orders a sergeant to break open a ballot box and do a "recount." Aureliano then joins the so-called Liberal forces which were in open rebellion about the countryside in trying to defeat the Conservatives on the battlefield of civil war. Violence is widespread. Social decomposition, nihilism, suicide, terrorism are rife. The Liberal rebellion is breaking up. Aureliano survives the government's massacre of his comrades. Now a colonel in the decimated Liberal army, Aureliano Buendía is a power holder. He escapes numerous ambushes and becomes commander-in-chief of Colombia's revolutionary forces; he is for a time the man the government fears most. He has power by violence and terror yet his disposition retains a certain unreal benevolence. Colonel Aureliano Buendía finally retires after the civil war is ended but refuses the lifetime pension the government offers him as a way of truce. He lives to old age manufacturing ornamental goldfish in a small shop in

Macondo, and admits that he has been fighting for personal pride more than for the Liberal cause.

All the while the banana company and the government continue to strangle Macondo socially and economically. Efforts to organize workers (whose complaints include labor on Sundays) are repressed with violence. Like straw soldiers the workers fall dead in the plaza before the army's war machine. There remains only a boy to recount the massacre at Macondo. But no one believes him as he tells his story wandering from village to village.

Then it rains for four years and some months. Macondo is inundated and left in shambles. The last Buendía, also named Aureliano, enters almost miraculously into a strange and incestuous relationship with his aunt whose husband abandoned her. Passion grows between this unlikely couple until at last the woman, Úrsula Amaranta, gives birth to a child who is born with the tail of a pig. At this instant the prophecy which Aureliano's father, founder of Macondo, received originally from the gypsy Melquíades comes true. The freak baby is devoured by ants, the mother dies, and the last Buendía wanders listlessly about the social maelstrom that is Macondo. At the precise moment in which he reads the final pages of the gypsy prophecy as to the village's final destiny, a deluge of rain covers everything and ends the life of Macondo.

This may be the way with much political life in Latin America, so the author seems to be telling us. Thus he explodes the notion of utopian panaceas generally. One cannot change his environment by dreaming. The constants of political life are power by physical threat, deceit, misfortune, and the curse of the supernatural. Democracy is a meaningless platitude used by politicians to deceive the people. Some of Macondo's inhabitants were migrants who came to escape their past, others came for adventure, all were potential aristocrats of a future society which was to be built. But in the end it was self-destructing. Macondo is cursed with utopian dreams that self-destruct every so-many years. It is political nostalgia, circular ideological voyages, a mirage of value anachronisms, physical horrors, igloos in a torrid zone that challenge a world without predictability. The author wants us to know that his vision is more than just Macondo, or Colombia. It is all of Latin America (and perhaps beyond).

García Márquez's literary license affords him flexibility in sketching a broad informal theory of Latin American society that includes socio-psychological, cultural, economic, political, and technological components unrestricted by disciplinary divisions or rigorous social scientific methodology. *One Hundred Years of Solitude* treats the contradictions and sometimes nonrational patterns of Latin American life without apology or effort to test hypotheses. To what extent does the myth of Macondo contribute to a model, a "Macondo syndrome" in the phenomenal sense, that can be used to explain much of the political atrophy in contemporary Latin America? Does such a literary construct do anything to clarify the study of politics and social change in the region?

Our purpose is to examine the political power-political democracy nexus which is at the heart of García

Márquez's novel. In exploring many issues raised by García Márquez we do not pretend to formalize or test an implicit theory. Rather our goal is to examine, as social scientists, a range of issues raised by the Colombian novelist and others of his ilk whose works may lay a basis for paradigm construction and eventual theory building. Accordingly, we will examine, selectively, some normative views of scholars (both North American and Latin American) on the questions of power and democracy and relate these to recent quantitative data of the reputational variety. Additionally our examination will include the interaction of power, democracy, and external (foreign) influences. . .all major components of Macondo. Macondo is a model of perpetual atrophy, a mosaic of discord, which may prepare one to accept if not approve the stagnation of political life in Latin America today and in the foreseeable future.

NORMATIVE THEORETIC DIMENSIONS

As in Macondo, elites in Latin American political life, their power sustained by exogenous influences (e.g., United States aid), are able to govern with practically unlimited repression. In the second half of the twentieth century repressive authoritarianism has increasingly dominated the politics of the southern half of the Western Hemisphere. Rebellion against such governing styles has also increased, a phenomenon known to some as insurgency and to others as national liberation. The result has been chronic instability and the cause of political democracy has been more frequently honored in word than by deed. The way power is used politically (in both the revolutionary and counterrevolutionary contexts) has serious implications for the development of political democracy.

A number of theorists have discussed revolution in terms of the "frustration-aggression hypothesis." This leads one to expect, according to James C. Davies, that "revolution is most likely to take place when there is a prolonged period of sharp reversal during which the gap between expectations and gratifications quickly widens and becomes intolerable."[1] Another way of putting this perhaps is to say that revolutions do not occur when people are totally desperate but when things are slightly improving. Eric Wolf argues much the same in saying that "revolt occurs not when men's faces are ground into the dust; rather, it explodes during a period of rising hope, at the point of sudden realization that only the traditional controls of the social order stand between men and the achievement of still greater hopes."[2] Similarly, in developing his psychological theory of "relative deprivation" Ted Robert Gurr observed that "only men who are enraged are likely to prefer violence despite the availability of effective nonviolent means for satisfying their expectations."[3]

But here is the nub of the dilemma of Latin America. By and large there are no "effective nonviolent means" nor indeed any means at all for solving one's problems. This was the plague of Macondo. But there are periods of rising hopes, like the return of Juan Perón to Argentina in 1973. And the atrophy of *peronism* unleashed a sustained period of insurgent violence, what Davies might consider a "period of short reversal." Also it is apparent that a large cross section of Latin American political ideologues are "enraged" to use Gurr's term *vis-à-vis* their socioeconomic and political milieu. It is difficult to determine the capacity of "the enraged" to threaten the *status quo* but, using a reputational technique which generates data of the "soft" variety, this study will explore the capacity or power of such groups to demand change as well as the ability of elite groups to resist it.

Although we may not be able to replicate it here, a classic dictum of Crane Brinton comes to mind: "Quantitatively, we may say that in a society markedly unstable there seem to be absolutely more intellectuals, at any rate comparatively more intellectuals, bitterly attacking existing institutions and desirous of a considerable alteration in society, business, and government."[4] This seems to be an adequate description of Latin America during most of the present century, and there is little evidence that the trend will be altered in the foreseeable future. The question remains as to how such conflicts will continue to be resolved, in the democratic arena of bargaining and compromise or via the gun or sword.

Our broad intent in this paper is to examine selectively some normative views of scholars (both North American and Latin American) on the question of the relationship between political power and political democracy in Latin America and to relate this to recent quantitative data of the reputational variety which may reflect on these concepts. Additionally we seek to examine the interaction between power, democracy and external assistance from the United States. Such foreign assistance or "aid" may be regarded as a kind of outside intervention in the workings of domestic Latin American political systems. This raises both ethical and practical questions about the nature of interventionism. We will consider, therefore, some of the more substantive human aspects of the interface between power, democracy, and aid, e.g., the collapse of Chilean and Uruguayan democracy during 1973. Events like these suggest the Macondo syndrome as an appropriate "model" for democratic collapse.

In the latter half of the twentieth century the term "power" as applied to Latin America tends to conjure up notions of dictatorship exercised by militarists and oligarchs who suppress popular liberation forces with violence. In at least three notable cases the drives of popular Latin American forces to overturn what was perceived as an archaic socioeconomic-political order were thwarted by external interventions from the United States. These were the cases of Guatemala (1954), the Dominican Republic (1965), and Chile (1973). Perhaps none of the interventions produced such reverberations within the North American political system as did a deliberate United States policy of undermining the constitutional government of Chile. This led to the death of President Salvador Allende and the massacre of thousands of Chilean citizens in a psychological and value crisis that can only partially be explained in terms of frustration and aggression or "gap theory" alone.

Clearly, we must distinguish between the "power" of a Latin American nation to guide its national destiny, order its internal affairs, and control the frustrations of its citizenry, from the "power" of foreigners to intervene and to manipulate, indeed to create frustrations and aggressions. Later we will present a somewhat refined definition of power that lends itself to reputational quantification within a cross-national context. A traditional definition of power that comprehends both domestic and external forces would be the ability to influence events, control behavior, and allocate values.

Historically the United States brought its power to bear on Latin American nations unilaterally, e.g., the war against Mexico (1845-48) and the seizure of Panama from Colombia in 1903. Throughout the first half of the twentieth century United States power was exercised throughout the Caribbean and Central America to keep the Europeans out and to establish "friendly" (which ultimately meant military) regimes. But in 1961 the majority of the Latin American nations and the United States joined together and subscribed to an ambitious plan known as the Alliance for Progress (ALPRO) which involved a multilateral commitment to exercise both domestic and external powers of influence. Among the ALPRO's goals were social justice, capitalistic economic development, a more equitable distribution of national wealth, eradication of illiteracy and poverty, plus the growth of nonviolent political democracy. Power was, ostensibly, to be shared democratically. We will concern ourselves here largely with the democratic component of the ALPRO's goals as a normative framework for the exercise of and competition for political, social, and economic power.

When the Alliance was put into motion in 1962 the majority of Latin American nations were governed by some sort of popularly elected constitutional government. Ten years later, when the Alliance "lost its way" and after over 20 billion dollars of U.S. investment, the majority of the area was under some form of dictatorship. The application of "linkage" politics had meant that the United States in effect undermined some of the goals to which it had originally subscribed. Either the United States intervened indirectly as in the cases of Brazil (1964) and Peru (1968) or the military aid received from the United States was used by local elites to stifle political development leading to democracy.

As we outlined the concept of democracy in Chapter One, by 1977 only Colombia, Costa Rica, and Venezuela had anything approaching democratic political systems. Second Era Peronism in Argentina had atrophied into such chaos that the military coup of March, 1976, was welcomed by most of the Argentine people. Uruguay, once the "Switzerland of the Americas," was under military rule as was nearly all of Central America. Mexico's president Echeverría decried outwardly that "emissaries of the past" were seeking to inspire a coup designed to end his nation's tradition of "single party democracy." He then climaxed his term in office by taking over *Excélsior*, the last national organ of press freedom his country enjoyed. So we may correctly ask throughout this study--what *is* political democracy and is this concept relevant to Latin American political life generally?[5]

There are those who question whether the ALPRO was meant to "democratize" the hemisphere. Some believe it was a cynical form of international blackmail and a disguised subsidy for United States interests. The writers Levinson and de Onís questioned the ability of the United States to underwrite repressive dictatorships about the hemisphere without calling the North American political system and its proclaimed democratic tenets into question.[6] Clearly there was an intricate and tenacious interface between power, democracy, and United States assistance policy in Latin America.

Much of United States aid policy to Latin America during the 1970 to 1976 period seems to have been based on postulates taken from the controversial "Rockefeller Report" of 1969, and these reflect directly on the issues of power and democracy. Specifically that report argued that through proper training the Latin American military sectors were being modernized and professionalized. In short:

> A new type of military man is coming to the fore and often becoming a major force for constructive social change in the American republics. Motivated by increasing impatience with corruption, inefficiency, and a stagnant political order, the new military man is prepared to adapt his authoritarian tradition to the goals of social and economic progress.[7]

With those words the "Rockefeller Report" implied a distinction between *political democracy* (as cited above in footnote 5) and *social democracy* emanating from human justice and opportunity within a framework of capitalistic economic growth, a point to which we shall return at the end of this treatise. The above statement carefully avoids saying that Latin American military men, trained in United States schools in the Panama Canal Zone and elsewhere, are abandoning their authoritarian tradition--just that they are adapting it to social and economic progress. It should be noted that when the Rockefeller fact-finding tour took place in 1969 such relatively democratic nations as Chile and Venezuela were unable to receive him due to public resentment against the United States. Rockefeller was received, however, by the Torrijos dictatorship in Panama (notoriously involved in narcotics traffic)[8] and by the Onganía dictatorship in Argentina (notorious for its repressive tactics against critics). Such regimes seem to have provided the prototype for Rockefeller's dictum quoted above. The belief that they are "progressive" has shaped United States policy during much of the 1970s.

This is not to deny some Latin militarists their due. Military regimes in 1976 such as those of Brazil, Ecuador, and Peru may be contributing to the economic development of their respective nations. We do, however, question whether such regimes are promoting the cause of social justice, human rights--what Christian Bay has called "potential freedom."[9] We also question whether Latin American regimes of any sort are truly becoming "impatient with corruption" and seeking to do something about it as the "Rockefeller Report" suggests. Such political corruption, as Samuel Huntington has argued, may be incompatible with true political development.[10]

Democratic political development would mean an expanded opportunity for more interests to exercise power, to make demands upon the system via legal means, without fear of reprisal and with reasonable hope of achieving some level of satisfaction. Example: frustration over continued electoral fraud and repression led Mexico's principal opposition party *Acción Nacional* to such internal disorder that it abstained from competition for the presidency in 1976. The party had no confidence that the system as constituted would yield any satisfactions *vis-à-vis* its members' interests.[11] Thus one could conclude that the cause of political development in Mexico had suffered. Indeed the ruling party acknowledged this when its spokesmen told the public that its real enemy was apathy and the "party of abstentionism" which threatened to discredit Mexican "democracy."[12] Space does not permit examples *ad infinitum*, but it would seem that overall political democracy declined throughout Latin America during the first half of the 1970s, the ALPRO notwithstanding.

We make the assumption in this essay that people without a social and/or economic stake in their nation are not likely to enjoy high levels of relevant political participation because they will have no culturally well rooted position of strength from which to demand such participation. Thus, the distinction between *power politics* and *participatory politics* becomes critical.

> Participatory politics is egalitarian: power politics is not. In the first case, citizens look horizontally to friends, associates, equals; in the second case, they look vertically to their government. The power state is inimical to commonwealth, if by commonwealth one means, as this essay does, a community sharing in certain vital responsibilities and privileges.[13]

The politics of power, which characterize most if not all of Latin America, do not lend themselves well to the resolution of conflict by nonviolent means. This is especially true when oligarchies are confronted not just by popular leaders but by renegade elitists turned populist. Colombia offers two excellent examples, the guerrilla priest Camilo Torres Restrepo and the renegade general Gustavo Rojas Pinilla, both of whom attracted an enormous popular following in defiance of their respective elite backgrounds. The politics of power is conducive to ideological cleavage and often generates violent attempts to settle disputes. On the other hand, for the politics of participation to operate effectively there must be some level of basic agreement, in the form of *enforceable* rules, on the manner in which political ideologues will agree and disagree. Obviously this requires toleration among those holding diverse and competing points of view. Political intolerance, usually arising from incompatible socioeconomic goals transposed into hostile political ideologies, characterizes the politics of Latin America generally and contributes to the defeat of participatory politics.

The quest for power in Latin America has led to a kind of "undemocracy," a "kleptocracy," in which leaders representing jealously guarded interests manipulate governments to serve selfish ends. Thus there are few who really *govern*; there are many who *command*. When "revolution" occurs it is most often no more than a *cuartelazo* in which nothing fundamental changes, only the incumbent stewards of power are pushed aside and replaced by other elites. Charles Anderson has given thorough treatment to the costs of entry and exit within the elite dominated political systems of Latin America,[14] but it is difficult to calculate the costs (i.e., risks) of forceful displacement of elites. This becomes especially perplexing in nations like Argentina, Bolivia, Ecuador, Honduras, and Peru which have recent histories that abound with military coups.

The politics of power is frequently dominated (in Latin America) by so-called "revolutionaries" (i.e., *golpistas*) who are often ill-equipped to use the power they have (or think they have) newly won.[15] Their tenure of office is therefore often short-lived. The people (under the politics of power) by and large look on from the sidelines at the machinations of elites struggling for more power and deference. The citizenry is usually forced to acquiesce in the manipulation of its life.

If a man considers all those outside his own *compadrazgo* to be potential enemies then he may contribute directly to making them into just that. It is common for Latin Americans to assume the unknown person to be "bad" until he proves himself to be "good." The early assumption is pejorative. Such a psychology does not lend itself to ideological tolerance; hence it discourages the growth of a participatory politics. Again Macondo dramatized this circumstance. The melancholy truth is, then, that participatory politics have been unable to penetrate most arenas of vital decision-making in Latin America to the extent that it has been possible in the Anglo-American cultures. Governmental elitism is protected by military and civilian bureaucratic organizations which claim monopolies over the use of coercive force, the use of economic sanctions, and ultimately over political legitimacy itself. The individual citizen's pursuit of power then becomes a matter of risking his own self-destruction, just as happened to the Buendías of Macondo.

There is a notable tendency for those whose quest for participation is frustrated to look toward utopian ideologies which offer identification and involvement at the outset but which also may demand unequivocal surrender in the end. Such may be the case with the *fidelista* movements about the hemisphere and the cult-oriented movements like the *peronistas* of Argentina. Latin America seems to be moving into a giant abyss between rulers and subjects which offers little hope for a true participatory politics. As unhampered population increase chokes nations with aspiring but thwarted minds and bodies, the eventuality of anarchy and destruction of the socioeconomic fabric becomes ever more real. National "liberation" movements are proliferating. In this sense, change may indeed be occurring, albeit via upheaval and violence.[16]

It is clear that a great amount of academic soil has been tilled by scholars who concern themselves with the direction of political change in Latin America. Martin Needler has devoted a stimulating book to the question of "development."[17] Another effort is that of Peter Ranis. He argues that a Latin American society in the process of political development needs a government that is *strong, compassionate,* and *just,* one which encourages *individual participation* and the "free and unfettered organization of a multitude of interests, and properly channelled discontent and opposition."[18] The normative bias of Ranis' position seems to be that political development (which we understand him to mean as change toward the Anglo-American variety of democratic practices) conduces to or is a thrust in the direction of political democracy, and moreover, that the ultimate outcome of this goal is "modernization." Perhaps we have misread Ranis, but he reiterates this in a concluding section: "The achievement of modernity requires a commitment to *pluralism, democracy,* and *rationally conceived social objectives* [our italics]. These values, however, require the increasing amelioration of social discontent."[19]

Ranis also tells us "central governments may have to make quick and forceful decisions which will raise revenue necessary for industrial expansion so that the increasing *employable* [our italics] population can be profitably absorbed."[20] Ranis eschews revolution as costly and too risky. He says there is emerging a "redistribution of power under the auspices of increasingly modern and progressive leadership [and that] it is often cheaper to modernize the military, clergy, and the landowners than to destroy them as economic and human resources."[21] That would seem to be a restatement of the fundamental bias of the "Rockefeller Report."

What Peter Ranis, the "Rockefeller Report," and other protagonists of conventional wisdom do not tell us is that the widespread abuse of public office, disregard for human rights and constitutional guarantees, and judicial systems turned into a burlesque all combine into a gigantic honesty vacuum of political kleptocracy, a Macondo throughout Latin America. Political leaders and public officials continue to be mostly responsible to their own narrowly defined interest group and *compadrazgo* loyalties. The public as a political constituency has yet to emerge in Latin America. That was to have been the achievement of Salvador Allende in Chile, but government by violence prevailed instead.[22] Value change toward honesty in politics and public administration is the most basic of all the requisites if Latin America is to move nearer to her oft professed but enigmatic goal of democratic political modernization. For if governments in Latin America continue to serve only their own narrow interests, and those of elite clientele groups, then there will be no "potential freedom" for anyone.[23]

In the Anglo-American version of the "modern state" it is assumed that an individual may gain personal satisfaction, even joy if he wishes, by involving himself politically in the basic decisions that affect his life. But for the Latin American citizen, the attempt for achievement for such "joy" may require that he risk his life in the overwhelming majority of cases. It is a matter of who has the capability to influence the decisions which determine his environment and, as we have stressed, to do so without fear of reprisals. The situations in the United States and Latin America are simply reversed in this respect. As Gary MacEoin has stated very effectively:

> One can estimate that in the United States approximately 20 percent of the people are so economically and culturally deprived that they lack the capacity to change or influence their environment. It is the other way around in Latin America. More than 80 percent of the people are not incorporated in any meaningful way into the national economies of their countries.[24]

By and large Latin American governments have also the power to order the execution and torture, Macondo style, of practically anyone who causes displeasure to the dominant elites. Even within countries which in the past have rated high on the Fitzgibbon Index[25] (e.g., Uruguay) there is a high incidence of officially sponsored brutality against critics of the incumbent regime. The right of public protest is severely curtailed throughout Latin America. Grass roots participation and institutionalized channels for making protests felt as well as merely heard, in the upper levels of the authority hierarchy are more myth than fact. There is little of what Alexander Groth has postulated:

> Democracy means elections and legislative assemblies; it means autonomous civic, political, and cultural associations and organs of expression. . .[it also means that] the democratic mode of behavior-- with its emphasis on dialogue and persuasion, rather than on suppression and annihilation. . .with its implicit recognition of the ultimate primacy of public opinion, not the judgment of a few--is likely to be appealing in and of itself to the individual whose psychocultural background, upbringing, and life experience predispose him for it.[26]

The lives of Latin Americans are torn by cycles of socioeconomic deprivation. These were not checked by the Alliance for Progress nor by other forms of United States interventionism. This impels many Latin Americans toward escapist panaceas including anarchy and, at the opposite extreme, acquiescence in authoritarianism and dictatorship. How the Latin American individual is raised, his instincts and expectations, his modes of thought and behavior, all determine his ability to contribute toward a national atmosphere in which political democracy can realistically be expected to thrive and not succumb to a pure power politics.

But does power really inhere in the existence of a political community as cited above (footnote 22) and, if so, is this compatible with the democratic process as we have set it forth conceptually herein? The survey data to be reported in the following chapters are offered with an eye to the list of democratic characteristics that appeared in Chapter One. We have stated earlier our broad understanding of power, i.e., the ability to influence events, control behavior, and allocate values--not an original definition by any means. More critically, we must distinguish between power and antidemocratic violence, the latter being chronic in Latin American political instability. Power and violence, of course, often go together, but no political community can exist without some sort of power (as Christian Bay, Hannah Arendt, and numerous others have argued). Power need not be justified, it is a natural phenomenon. Violence, on the other hand, is an aberration and must be justified as an extension of legitimate power when used. That is to say, power can be legitimized but does not need to be justified. Violence may be justified, but can never be legitimized (this according to Hannah Arendt).

In Latin America of the 1970s Macondo-style politics with power exercised through antidemocratic violence is common. And when legitimate power is replaced by violence (as, many will say, is true today in Brazil, Chile, Haiti, Nicaragua, and elsewhere) then the inevitable result is terror, i.e., "the form of government that comes into being when violence, having destroyed all power, does not abdicate but, on the contrary, remains in full control."[27] This sounds very much like a cryptic restatement of the Macondo syndrome. Violence has become a way of political "life" in certain Latin American countries and this cannot but influence the scholarly image of democracy therein. Power via antidemocratic violence is a culture-relative factor that must condition our examination of the democratic process (or its absence) throughout Latin America. Later we will even entertain the possibility that some traditionally democratic functions like public accountability and rotation in office might be performed by violent and what are also traditionally viewed as undemocratic means.

FOOTNOTES: CHAPTER TWO

1. James C. Davies, "The J-Curve of Rising and Declining Satisfactions as a Cause of Some Great Revolutions and a Contained Rebellion," as quoted in Anne E. Freedman and P. E. Freedman, *The Psychology of Political Control* (New York: St. Martin's Press, 1975), p. 166.

2. Eric R. Wolf, *Sons of the Shaking Earth* (Chicago: University of Chicago Press, 1959), pp. 108-9.

3. Ted Robert Gurr, *Why Men Rebel* (Princeton: Princeton University Press, 1970), p. 317.

4. From Crane Brinton's *The Anatomy of Revolution,* 1952, as reprinted in Roy Macridis and Bernard Brown, eds., *Comparative Politics: Notes and Readings,* 5th ed. (Homewood: Dorsey Press, 1961), p. 176.

5. One statement of the concept "political democracy" that is based on the works of a number of theorists appears in Kenneth F. Johnson, "Scholarly Images of Latin American Political Democracy in 1975," *Latin American Research Review,* 11, 2 (Summer 1976), 129-41. His formulation stresses a series of human freedom elements, the ability of pluralistic groups to challenge the *status quo* without fear of reprisal, and impartial rules which guide the exercise of popular sovereignty by benevolent, as opposed to exploitive, governments.

6. See Simon G. Hanson, *Dollar Diplomacy Modern Style* (Washington, D.C.: Inter-American Affairs Press, 1970), passim; and Jerome Livingston and Juan de Onís, *The Alliance that Lost its Way* (New York: Quadrangle Books, 1970), p. 324.

7. *Quality of Life in the Americas* (Report of a U.S. Presidential Mission for the Western Hemisphere under the signature of Nelson A. Rockefeller) (Washington, D.C.: USAID, 1969), p. 18. The report admits in its foreword (cf. p.v) that the Alliance for Progress was a failure and later reflects upon the question of political democracy saying, "democracy is a very subtle and difficult problem for most of the other countries in the hemisphere. The authoritarian and hierarchical tradition which has conditioned and formed the cultures of most of these societies does not lend itself to the particular kind of popular government we are used to. Few of these countries, moreover, have achieved the sufficiently advanced economic and social systems required to support a consistently democratic system. For many of these societies, therefore, the question is less one of democracy or a lack of it, than it is simply of orderly ways of getting along"(p. 46). The bias implicit here, of course, is that with continued U.S. investment for "development" socioeconomic systems will one day become "modern" and spawn democracy. At that point, however, as in the case of Chile (1973) a democratically supported and arrived at decision to nationalize U.S. investments may be-

come too much democracy for the U.S. to tolerate. And then the United States would have to undo its own democratic "creation" as, indeed, happened in Chile.

8. Evidence of the Panamanian government's narcotics involvement can be found in U.S. Congress, House, Report on Activities during the 92nd Congress of the Committee on Merchant Marine and Fisheries (92nd Congress, Second Session), H. Rept. 92-1629 (1973), p. 29.

9. Bay has written, "An individual's potential freedom, or the relative absence of unperceived external restraints on his behavior, is necessarily limited by all institutions that he unwittingly internalizes or takes for granted. It follows that a "complete" potential freedom is an absurdity and that the problem of maximizing potential freedom requires some specification as to the types of restraints that should be maximized. . .(and). . .for the potential freedom of the individual, on the other hand, the difference between high and low degrees of institutionalization is more important than the difference between democracy and dictatorship." Bay is greatly concerned with manipulations of individual destinies of which the given persons may not be aware and says "Slaves of customs may be as unfree as the slaves of dictators." From *The Structure of Freedom* (New York: Atheneum, 1968), pp. 315, 317, and 353.

10. See his *Political Order in Changing Societies* (New Haven: Yale University Press, 1968), pp. 59-69, passim.

11. In point of fact, the PAN was subject to such internal pressures stemming from demoralization in its ranks following a series of government engineered electoral frauds that it was unable to agree upon a presidential candidate in 1976 and ultimately voted to abstain.

12. Daniel Cosío Villegas, *El estilo personal de gobernar* (México: Cuadernos de Joaquín Mortiz, 1974), p. 78.

13. Robert J. Pranger, *The Eclipse of Citizenship* (New York: Holt-Rinehart-Winston, 1968), p. 29.

14. See his *Politics and Economic Change in Latin America* (Princeton: Van Nostrand, 1967), especially pp. 105-112.

15. See F. LaMond Tullis, *Politics and Social Change in Third World Countries* (New York: Wiley, 1973), p. 70.

16. See T. Lynn Smith, *The Race Between Population and Food Supply in Latin America* (Albuquerque: University of New Mexico Press, 1976), for a somewhat more optimistic view of this problem.

17. See *Political Development in Latin America* (New York: Random House, 1968).

18. Peter Ranis, *Five Latin American Nations* (New York: Macmillan, 1971), p. 5.

19. Ranis, p. 281.
20. Ranis, p. 285.
21. Ranis, p. 323.
22. Hannah Arendt has written that power is inherent in the existence of a political community but violence is not. Power need not be justified; violence, used as an extension of power, must be justified but can never be legitimized permanently. Terror, then, is that form of government when violence destroys all legitimate power and assumes full control. See her *On Violence* (New York: Harcourt, Brace, & World, 1970), pp. 52-55.
23. As cited from Bay above, this relates to the overall freedom of the individual from coercion, either perceived or latent, and his ability to develop as he chooses.
24. Gary MacEoin, *Revolution Next Door* (New York: Holt-Rinehart-Winston, 1971), p. 17.
25. See "Scholarly Images. . ." (footnote five) for discussion of the Fitzgibbon technique.
26. Alexander J. Groth, *Comparative Politics: A Distributive Approach* (New York: Macmillan, 1971), pp. 26 and 37.
27. Hannah Arendt, *On Violence* (footnote 22), p. 52.

CHAPTER THREE
MEASURING THE SCHOLARLY IMAGE DEMOCRACY IN LATIN AMERICA

THEORETICAL AND METHODOLOGICAL UNDERPINNINGS[1]

Political democracy is commonly conceptualized in terms of an Anglo-American model emphasizing "popular suffrage" and "parliamentary government." Widespread acceptance of this notion has not alleviated the difficulty of moving from an ideal type to an empirical classification, however. The democratic label tends to attach the aura of legitimacy to the regime in power and is, therefore, widely used and abused. More than one authoritarian has constructed the façade of democratic institutions and processes to gain domestic and international respectability. Operationalizing democracy is made even more difficult when such issues as "one man, one vote" are raised. The abstractness and normative connotations associated with the concept contribute greatly to the "dissensus" in its operationalization and has resulted in a myriad of approaches. We have refrained from the temptation to formulate still another operational definition of political democracy and have opted instead for a description of what we consider to be the essential components, drawing freely from the ideas of Leslie Lipson.[2] As we stated it in Chapter One, political democracy requires essentially the following: popular sovereignty exercised through competing interest groups that vie for power and leadership within a fixed and impartial set of rules that are applied evenly and impartially to all participants; that the state and its personnel exist to serve the public as their primary constituency, i.e., the state does not rob the people nor do the people rob the state as "amoral familists" could be expected to do if we embrace Banfield's "predictive" hypothesis[3]; that there be some free and honest procedure for selecting leaders of the state that will be competitive and popular; that the leadership elements so selected will be perpetually (or at least periodically) subject to public review, challenge and/or removal, again within an impartial set of guidelines; that the stakes in the power struggle not be so high as to make it impossible for one politically relevant participant group to accept an adverse popular judgment vis-à-vis its candidate or favored policy (here is one of the critical areas of breakdown of political democracy in Latin America, for given the extreme polarization of ideological cleavage that has existed, and accompanying zero-sum game conditions of the power struggle for scarce resources, the stakes in most countries are simply too high for the power contenders to allow an impartial popular decision to occur; hence, military interventions or other manifestations of extra-legality have been widespread).

Assuming that one could operationalize this conceptualization of democracy in such a manner that "hard" data could be gathered cross-nationally (probably an unrealistic assumption) we suspect that virtually all cases would fall into the nondemocratic column, thus reducing or eliminating the value of the concept. Methodologically, it may make more sense to develop measures using an ideal type as a guideline and then to compare countries ordinarily along an observable continuum.

In 1945, Russell H. Fitzgibbon initiated what was to become a controversial yet provocative series of quinquennial experiments designed to measure democratic change in Latin America. Controversy developed both because of the nature of the data base and the variables selected. Fitzgibbon did not use "hard" data to measure democracy or democratic change; rather he called on scholars to evaluate twenty Latin American countries using criteria he set forth. In effect Fitzgibbon was measuring the *scholarly image* of democracy in the hemisphere rather than democracy itself. Recognizing the importance of the distinction and the caution one should exercise in interpreting "soft" data of this sort, the quinquennial experiments are significant and important for several reasons. First, the *perception* of democracy rather than an *objective presence* (analogous to the distinction between relative and objective deprivation)[4] serves as the basis of legitimacy and individual political action. Thus we find governments such as the military regime in Brazil artificially creating and maintaining a two-party system to foster the illusion of popular suffrage, popular participation and parliamentary government. The purpose is to enhance international respectability and increase regime legitimacy. The Fitzgibbon Index has become significant as a continuous time-series spanning a period of thirty years. We know of no other time-series in Latin America or elsewhere that affords scholars a comparable opportunity to examine democratic change or the image of democratic change.

The technique developed by Fitzgibbon is comparatively simple and has its defects and limitations. A panel of specialists on Latin America, including scholars and journalists, is asked to rank each country in Latin America with respect to fifteen criteria that are considered to reflect the principal components of democracy. Each rank (using the letters A, B, C, D, and E) is judged against the ideal rather than a ranking of countries for each criterion. The letter scores are then converted to numerical scores which are tabulated for each item in each country. The result is a country-item matrix twenty rows by fifteen columns plus totals. From this basic matrix a number of statistical comparisons are made.

Many have correctly argued that not all items in the Fitzgibbon Index are political. Therefore, some have urged that they be eliminated or replaced.[5] To do so, of course, would destroy the comparability of the surveys and so the decision was made to preserve the items in future surveys. The validity of the criticism was recognized, however, and Johnson consulted a number of colleagues on possible improvements short of changing the basic format. Based in part on the constructive criticism of Merle Kling and James Wilkie, five items from the original index were singled out for special attention and analysis. These items more directly reflect the conceptualization of *political* democracy outlined above. Additionally, these items are more familiar to respondents and therefore easier to score. In the subsequent analysis of the seven quinquennial surveys, the five-item index of political democracy will be the subject of our investigation unless otherwise stated.

Additional criticism of the technique has centered on the lack of uniform standards of subjective judgment used to evaluate each criterion in each country by a diverse panel of scholars. This does pose a potential problem of course, and one which Fitzgibbon and Johnson have noted and attempted to minimize. In this regard a conscious effort to recruit panelists from across the ideological spectrum has been made. This as well as the increased size of the panel in recent surveys and the aggregating of responses has been done with the purpose of reducing extreme bias.

The growing size of the panel has made it necessary to adjust the raw scores of each survey to achieve comparability. The equalized raw scores were computed to account for the expanding panel. Following the 1975 survey a new technique was developed by Miles Williams in collaboration with Johnson to examine the seven surveys as a time-series. Rather than raw scores or equalized raw scores as in the past, a Democratic Rating Coefficient (DRC) is computed for each indicator in each country. The basic advantage of the DRC over previous scoring systems is that it not only allows for comparisons between surveys, as does the equalized raw scoring system, but it also permits ready comparison between DRC scores and a minimum/maximum value. Since the numerical scoring system has a range of 1 to 5 (rather than 0 to 4) for each item, the range of the DRC coefficients is .20 to 1.0 (rather than 0 to 1.0).

In essence the DRC is simply the raw score divided by the maximum possible score. The maximum possible score is computed by multiplying the number of respondents by the maximum possible response (always 5). If one is calculating the maximum possible score for each country, one multiplies the number of respondents by the maximum possible response (5) by the number of items (either 5 or 15, depending on whether one is using the original Fitzgibbon Index or the 5-item index of political democracy). Finally, if one is calculating a coefficient for each item, he multiplies the number of respondents by the maximum possible response (5) per respondent by the number of countries. The resulting DRCs afford a comparison of countries and items for each year as well as a comparison over time, all against a maximum possible score.

THE CHANGING SCHOLARLY IMAGE OF DEMOCRACY IN LATIN AMERICA

On the whole the seven image index surveys offer a gloomy picture of democracy in Latin America, particularly since 1960. The decline in the image of democracy between 1970 and 1975 was to be expected given the military takeovers in Chile and Uruguay, but an even greater decline, measured here by the Democratic Rating Coefficients, occurred between 1965 and 1970. Coincidentally or not, this occurred in the wake of the Dominican intervention by the United States in 1965 and a general disaffection with the Alliance for Progress. The strong revival of democracy in the late fifties did not carry over into the sixties as the hemisphere seemed to react to the Cuban revolution with

FIGURE 1

SUBSTANTIVE CRITERIA OF THE FITZGIBBON-JOHNSON IMAGE INDEX

Items Included in Original
Fitzgibbon Index*

Select Criteria Used in
Examination of Political Democracy

1. Educational level
2. Standard of living
3. Internal unity
4. Political maturity
5. Freedom from foreign domination
6. Freedom of press, speech, etc.
7. Free elections
8. Freedom of political organization
9. Independent judiciary
10. Handling of government funds
11. Social legislation
12. Degree of civilian supremacy
13. Freedom from ecclesiastical domination
14. Governmental administration
15. Local government autonomy

6. Freedom of press, speech, etc.
7. Free elections
8. Freedom of political organization
9. Independent judiciary

12. Degree of civilian supremacy

*Each respondent was given a brief statement of how each criterion should be understood (in more or less terms) so as to give something of a common frame of reference to all the responding scholars. The problems of conceptual and substantive overlap in this index have been acknowledged in the light of published criticisms of the technique, and all of this is dealt with in Kenneth F. Johnson, "Measuring the Scholarly Image of Latin American Democracy: 1945-1970," in James Wilkie and Paul Turovsky, eds., *Statistical Abstract of Latin America* (Los Angeles: UCLA Latin American Center, 1976).

Source: Kenneth F. Johnson, "Scholarly Images of Latin American Political Democracy," *Latin American Research Review*, 11:2 (Summer 1976), 129-41.

tighter political controls. The Latin American experience since World War II seems to fit the cyclical pattern of democracy leading to open demands for reform leading to military intervention followed by renewed interest in democracy, and so on.[6] The quinquennial studies reflect this pattern clearly, illustrating that the scholarly image of democracy in Latin America showed general improvement from 1945 through 1960 but beyond that point the region experienced a sharp decline which continues today.

Judging from the scholarly images of Latin American life, not all aspects of the hemispheric condition have experienced major fluctuations. In fact, some social and economic items in the fifteen-item index, e.g., educational level and standard of living, have remained comparatively unchanged. The five items in the political democracy index have experienced the greatest range of response ("free elections," followed by "freedom of press," "civilian supremacy," "party organization," and "independent judiciary,"). This, of course, is reflected in the greater variability of the five-item index than for the original fifteen-item index developed by Fitzgibbon.

By their very nature political institutions and processes are vulnerable to rapid change. Constitutions, for example, are founded on normative assumptions (not always accepted by large sectors of the population), and outline procedures for dealing with social conflict by prescribing who authoritatively allocates values and to whom political incumbents are accountable. The stability of these institutions and processes depends largely on the continued support for these guiding principles by those in a position to exert power or influence. Charles Anderson's classic model of the Latin American political process suggests that voting, like all demonstrable "power capabilities," may be utilized by power contenders in their quest for a decision-making role in the political process, but that it (voting) is not necessarily definitive.[7] The fact that democratic capabilities are at best tentative determinants of the power contender's role accents the problem of democratic persistence in Latin America. The tragic cases of Chile and Uruguay in 1973 illustrate clearly that even those societies with long-standing democratic traditions are vulnerable and that the demise of democratic institutions and processes tends to be quick and total. A strong democratic political culture may dissuade some would-be autocrats from challenging those with democratic "power capabilities," but a millennium of parliamentary government does not cushion the fall when constitutional governments are in fact overthrown.

Social and economic stability is less dependent on psychological commitments. The immediate impact of a major political upheaval on the level of education is not likely to be too great. Even the standard of living may not be affected by political change in the short run. Social and economic conditions are more a result of objective, concrete achievements than the state of mind of society's influentials. This fact, of course, creates its own set of problems. While incumbent power holders (democratic or otherwise) are always faced with the prospect of having to relinquish power quickly, those same individuals (and their challengers) are comparatively ineffectual when

TABLE 1

DEMOCRATIC RATING COEFFICIENT (DRC) FOR SEVEN FITZGIBBON-JOHNSON IMAGE INDEX STUDIES
(1945-1975)

	1945 15-Items	1945 5-Items	1950 15-Items	1950 5-Items	1955 15-Items	1955 5-Items	1960 15-Items	1960 5-Items	1965 15-Items	1965 5-Items	1970 15-Items	1970 5-Items	1975 15-Items	1975 5-Items
Argentina	.75	.62	.67	.42	.63	.37	.83	.84	.79	.76	.62	.45	.67	.65
Bolivia	.36	.32	.39	.46	.46	.46	.52	.56	.48	.48	.49	.46	.40	.37
Brazil	.59	.48	.72	.74	.75	.80	.76	.80	.69	.67	.54	.41	.54	.36
Chile	.83	.88	.85	.92	.83	.90	.86	.93	.88	.95	.80	.86	.51	.31
Colombia	.78	.88	.71	.70	.61	.54	.75	.82	.74	.82	.68	.75	.71	.82
Costa Rica	.85	.92	.82	.88	.88	.93	.90	.95	.91	.96	.80	.85	.85	.93
Cuba	.70	.73	.76	.84	.62	.54	.56	.41	.48	.29	.50	.29	.63	.38
Domin. Republic	.39	.30	.42	.25	.39	.24	.41	.23	.51	.49	.52	.55	.50	.54
Ecuador	.47	.48	.54	.65	.56	.64	.64	.74	.53	.55	.56	.61	.48	.43
El Salvador	.51	.45	.52	.44	.56	.56	.60	.59	.60	.60	.55	.55	.52	.50
Guatemala	.47	.43	.56	.57	.47	.45	.55	.62	.52	.51	.51	.55	.45	.44
Haiti	.39	.40	.41	.39	.45	.44	.38	.36	.31	.26	.32	.27	.30	.27
Honduras	.39	.36	.46	.42	.58	.53	.53	.57	.51	.49	.49	.49	.42	.40
Mexico	.64	.62	.68	.65	.76	.76	.79	.78	.80	.79	.72	.71	.72	.73
Nicaragua	.42	.37	.44	.33	.42	.31	.46	.37	.51	.46	.48	.44	.40	.35
Panama	.62	.69	.56	.57	.59	.60	.61	.66	.63	.70	.49	.45	.51	.43
Paraguay	.37	.33	.36	.32	.36	.33	.36	.27	.41	.32	.44	.35	.38	.30
Peru	.57	.58	.52	.43	.46	.35	.65	.73	.64	.71	.55	.51	.54	.39
Uruguay	.90	.93	.91	.94	.97	.99	.91	.96	.91	.96	.79	.84	.64	.51
Venezuela	.59	.62	.55	.48	.50	.36	.72	.77	.77	.83	.74	.80	.80	.88
Latin America	.58	.57	.59	.57	.59	.56	.64	.65	.63	.63	.58	.56	.55	.50

TABLE 2

RATING COEFFICIENTS OF 15 ITEMS FOR ALL COUNTRIES
USED IN FITZGIBBON-JOHNSON IMAGE INDEX EXPERIMENTS
(1945-1975)

	1945	1950	1955	1960	1965	1970	1975
Educational Level	.52	.58	.57	.59	.61	.58	.59
Standard of Living	.53	.56	.56	.57	.57	.55	.55
Internal Unity	.62	.64	.63	.67	.64	.63	.65
Political Maturity	.56	.59	.59	.62	.62	.58	.56
Freedom from For. Dom.	.66	.67	.70	.73	.73	.61	.59
*Freedom of Press, etc.	.65	.61	.61	.69	.68	.59	.52
*Free Elections	.55	.54	.55	.66	.63	.54	.48
*Party Organization	.53	.55	.53	.64	.63	.55	.51
*Judiciary	.57	.58	.55	.62	.62	.57	.51
Governmental Funds	.53	.55	.55	.59	.60	.56	.55
Social Legislation	.56	.61	.62	.63	.63	.59	.59
*Civilian Supremacy	.57	.57	.53	.63	.60	.55	.48
Ecclesiastical Freedom	.75	.72	.73	.74	.76	.71	.67
Governmental Admin.	.55	.56	.57	.62	.59	.57	.56
Local Government	.54	.55	.55	.59	.56	.52	.49

*Items included in the select criteria of political democracy.

it comes to producing rapid improvement in the objective social and economic condition. The level of education cannot be immediately increased (nor decreased) by edict, nor can the overall level of economic development, although a redistribution of the wealth (poverty) may be accomplished in a fairly short revolutionary period.

In the final analysis there is a direct relationship between the potential instability of political institutions and processes and the comparative stability of social and economic conditions. The resources or power capabilities of competing power contenders may depend on their constituents' perception of how values are authoritatively allocated and with what result. Yet the ability of power holders to bring about objective change in social and economic conditions in the short run is highly limited. As Tables 1 and 2 indicate, the scholarly image of social and economic conditions in Latin America over the past thirty years has been minimal while the image of change in political institutions and processes has been substantial.

The political currency of power contenders in Latin America and elsewhere is the promise of a better life. As García Márquez suggests in *One Hundred Years of Solitude*, utopian panaceas like the promise of participatory democracy leading to a better life are cruel because they raise expectations which, when dashed, seem to be followed by a high incidence of political repression. While estimates of political executions and detention are probably unreliable, fragmentary reports would appear to support the proposition that a strong relationship exists between a high DRC, high DRC variability, and the incidence of extreme political repression.

Table 3 shows both the thirty-year average democratic rankings and ratings as well as the variability around the mean over the seven surveys. It is evident that a high overall democratic rating is not a reliable indicator of low variability (high system stability) of democratic conditions. Ideally, one might hope that the more democratic countries would also be those countries in which institutions and processes would be the least vulnerable to great fluctuations. However, such is not the case and the weak rho score of .20 suggests that authoritarian institutions and processes are about as entrenched in some countries as democracy is in others. Of the ten countries with the highest thirty-year democratic ratings, six were below the median rankings of low variability. Costa Rica and to a lesser extent Colombia and Mexico were the only countries that consistently have had high democratic ratings since 1945.

TABLE 3

THE CHANGING SCHOLARLY IMAGE OF DEMOCRACY IN LATIN AMERICA
(1945-1975)

Mean DRC*	Country	30 Year Rank	Coefficient of Variability**	Rank (least)	Change in 1975 DRC from Mean
.92	Costa Rica	1	.035	1	+.01
.88	Uruguay	2	.267	15	-.37
.80	Chile	3	.265	14	-.59
.76	Colombia	4	.132	5	+.06
.72	Mexico	5	.117	3	+.01
.69	Brazil	6	.283	18	-.32
.68	Venezuela	7	.268	16	+.20
.59	Argentina	8	.282	17	+.06
.59	Ecuador	9	.169	10	-.16
.54	Peru	10	.177	11	-.15
.53	Panama	11	.219	13	-.10
.53	El Salvador	12	.119	4	-.03
.51	Guatemala	13	.139	7	-.07
.50	Cuba	14	.400	20	-.12
.47	Honduras	15	.151	8	-.07
.44	Bolivia	16	.161	9	-.07
.38	Nicaragua	17	.134	6	-.03
.37	Dom. Republic	18	.373	19	-.17
.34	Haiti	19	.209	12	-.07
.32	Paraguay	20	.047	2	+.02

* The mean DRCs are rounded off in this table, thus accounting for the absence of ties in rankings.

** The coefficient of variability, like standard deviation, allows one to measure variation among cases. Differing mean values (in this case one for each country over thirty years) are more likely to produce misleading coefficients when the standard deviation is used than when the coefficient of variability is calculated; hence, the coefficient of variability was selected.

If the prospect for future democracy in a Latin American society is not significantly improved by a lengthy, unbroken past experience with democracy, and the evidence (particularly from Chile and Uruguay) indicates that it is not, then what are the correlates of democracy and system stability? Figure 2, based on rho scores from the average rank of selected items from the fifteen-item index and Table 3, indicates a strong positive relationship between those same socioeconomic items and political democracy, but a negative relationship between those same socioeconomic conditions and system stability. Only social legislation was positively (if weakly) associated with system stability. *Thus, while these selected indicators of "modernization" were strongly correlated with political democracy, these same indicators were negatively correlated with system stability as was political democracy, though weakly.* If indeed this scholarly image reflects the reality, or even the Latin American power contenders' perception of the reality, then can one reasonably expect Latin American leaders to sincerely pursue democratic objectives? Is this not a statistical reflection (simulation?) of Macondo?

On the other hand, authoritarian political systems have attempted to project an image of social reform in recent years. The Peruvian military takeover of 1968 is illustrative. The military intervention was justified to the people in large part by the need for fundamental reform within the context of political stability, a stability that was thought to be threatened by guerrilla activity in the mid-sixties and the constant if ineffectual presence of the Apristas. Thus the military assumed control and promptly expropriated rich farmland owned by the Grace Corporation as well as the International Petroleum Company's holdings. This was followed by an extensive agrarian reform program. With this the military could gain control, establish (authoritarian) stability, assume the role of reformer without seriously affecting the Peruvian national socioeconomic structures. In 1965, the last quinquennial survey before the 1968 military takeover, the Peruvian DRC was .71 while the rating coefficient for social legislation was .62. The DRC in 1975 had declined to .39 but the rating coefficient for social legislation had risen to .76.

The Panamanian pattern has been less dramatic but has followed the same general lines in recent years. Since 1965 the image of Panamanian democracy has declined while the social legislation rating coefficient has remained generally steady. Increasingly, military regimes and non-leftist civilian regimes (e.g., Venezuela, Colombia, and Mexico) have gone to some length to project a liberal, reformist image. Venezuela, Colombia and Mexico have been among those countries advocating closer relations with Cuba and independence from the United States. Venezuela nationalized oil and has been negotiating economic agreements with the Soviet Union; Colombian President Alfonso López was elected on a platform of income redistribution; and former Mexican President Luis Echeverría's final act as that nation's chief executive was to grant the peasants large parcels of land. While basic social reform has not characterized any of these civilian regimes in recent

Different contenders obviously possess differing kinds of capabilities and the society's potential for political democracy will depend in large part on which groups are best able to utilize their respective capabilities at any given time.

In the following chapter selected power contenders will be examined and compared in the twenty Latin American states. Based on a supplemental instrument developed for the 1975 quinquennial survey, the image of the existing power capabilities possessed by contending groups will be explored. With this, another dimension of the image of democracy and the potential for democracy in the hemisphere should emerge.

FOOTNOTES: CHAPTER THREE

1. Material for this section is based in large part on Kenneth F. Johnson, "Scholarly Images of Latin American Political Democracy," *Latin American Research Review* 11, 2 (Summer 1976); and Johnson, "Measuring the Scholarly Image of Latin American Democracy: 1945-1970," in James Wilkie, ed., *Statistical Abstract of Latin America, 1976* (Los Angeles: UCLA, 1976).

2. Leslie Lipson, *The Democratic Civilization* (New York: Oxford University Press, 1964), particularly p. 589.

3. Edward Banfield, *The Moral Basis of a Backward Society* (New York: The Free Press, 1958).

4. Ted Robert Gurr, *Why Men Rebel* (Princeton: Princeton University Press, 1970).

5. See Johnson, "Measuring the Scholarly Image," for a discussion of the pros and cons involved in the decision to "save" the time-series from those who would have junked it altogether.

6. Edwin Lieuwin, *Generals Vs. Presidents: Nonmilitarism in Latin America* (New York: Fredrick A. Praeger, 1964).

CHAPTER FOUR
THE POLITICAL DEMOCRACY-POLITICAL POWER NEXUS

INTRODUCTION

Democratic institutions do not accumulate stability ascriptively over consecutive years of representative government as we noted in our examination of the seven quinquennial surveys in the previous chapter. Certainly one might reasonably expect a country with fifty years of successful democratic experience to have a higher probability of continued representative government than one with five years. Yet as the cases of Chile and Uruguay in 1973 illustrate, there are no guarantees; conversely, as the case of post-1957 Venezuela demonstrates, a country with a history of authoritarian regimes is also capable of reversing that pattern.

Scholars have noted that in Latin America there exists "an imperfect consensus on the nature of the political regime"[1] and suggest that most of the political leadership in Latin America does not view constitutional processes as the last word in determining that leadership. Elections are simply one means of demonstrating a "power capability" but by no means the only source of influence or power. The ability to mobilize the military, arouse the population to revolt, as well as any number of other options, may be considered viable by power contenders. In Latin America as elsewhere the question is not whether there exist political elites but rather the magnitude of their power capabilities *vis-à-vis* each other and, in democracies, whether or not "ordinary citizens exert a relatively high degree of control over leaders. . . ."[2]

In the previous chapter we examined the scholarly image of democracy in Latin America and, implicitly, the question of citizen control over leaders. In this chapter we will broach the question of the power capabilities of selected power contenders in the twenty Latin American states. We will also examine the relationship between political democracy and the power capabilities of the various contenders.

The 1975 Fitzgibbon-Johnson instrument was supplemented by a power index which was presented to the panel of scholars and was to be scored in exactly the same manner as the fifteen items originally developed by Fitzgibbon. A Power Rating Coefficient (PRC) was computed using the same technique as for the Democratic Rating Coefficient (DRC) described in the previous chapter. When the power index was presented to the panel, it was instructed that:

> For purposes of this experiment, political power is defined as the ability of individuals, groups, or interest sectors to influence public behavior, control events, allocate values (all in prized situations having public relevance as perceived by given actors, groups and/or sectors). This includes not only formal access which a given group or influence sector may have to the legal

institutions of decision-making, *but also* includes such extra-legal avenues of influence as informal pressure activities, religious influences, personal working relationships, paramilitary activities, terrorism and guerilla warfare, and so on.

The categories of actors in the power index included foreign interests, landed oligarchy, industrialists, *campesinado*, urban proletariat, military establishment, and anti-government insurgents. While these seven groups obviously do not exhaust the possible range of power contenders in Latin America, they do at least tap major competing sectors, e.g., urban versus rural, business versus labor, foreign versus domestic, large landowners versus peasants, civilians versus military as well as church versus secular authority and establishment versus insurgents.

THE POWER RATING COEFFICIENT

Table 4 clearly indicates that the traditional elites (i.e., landed oligarchy, foreign interests, military establishment, industrialists, and the Church) are still perceived to be the dominant political forces in Latin America. The military was seen as possessing the greatest power capabilities followed by foreign interests and landed oligarchy, and to a much lesser extent, the Church.

That the military and foreign interests should be viewed as dominant is not surprising, as virtually the entire hemisphere is under military control. Moreover, since 1949 the United States Army School of the Americas in the Panama Canal Zone has graduated over 30,000 Latin American military personnel and of these better than 180 have gone on to head governments, serve as cabinet ministers, become commanding generals, chiefs of staff, or directors of intelligence.[3] More will be said about the military and foreign interests in the following chapter.

Several noteworthy patterns emerge when we compare the PRCs within and between countries. First, in fourteen of the twenty countries the military establishment had higher PRCs than any of the other selected political sector actors. Industrialists rated higher in Venezuela, Mexico, and Colombia; foreign interests rated highest in Costa Rica; the landed oligarchy in El Salvador; and, the urban proletariat in Argentina where Peronism lingers on. The relative power of industrialists and landed oligarchy was directly related to the standard of living in the Fitzgibbon Index. In eight of the ten highest ranking countries on the standard of living item, industrialists were perceived to be more powerful than the landed oligarchy. Conversely, in the ten lowest ranking countries on the same item, only once were industrialists seen as more powerful than the landed oligarchy; that was in Peru. The Peruvian military's "revolution," which has included a verbal commitment to land reform, may account for the ostensibly deviant Peruvian case.

Foreign interests and landed oligarchy were thought to be more powerful than industrialists in most Central American-Caribbean countries including the Dominican Republic, El Salvador, Guatemala, Haiti, Honduras,

TABLE 4
POWER RATING COEFFICIENTS (PRC) OF SELECTED POLITICAL ACTORS IN LATIN AMERICA (1975)

	Argentina	Bolivia	Brazil	Chile	Colombia	Costa Rica	Cuba	Dom. Rep.	Ecuador	El Salvador	Guatemala	Haiti	Honduras	Mexico	Nicaragua	Panama	Paraguay	Peru	Uruguay	Venezuela	Latin America
Foreign Interests	.63	.77	.74	.78	.69	.72	.73	.87	.75	.78	.83	.78	.83	.68	.84	.83	.74	.59	.71	.67	.75
Landed Oligarchy	.72	.61	.74	.74	.77	.68	.22	.86	.86	.92	.90	.77	.89	.61	.92	.76	.87	.60	.75	.67	.75
Industrialists	.78	.60	.88	.88	.82	.71	.29	.72	.72	.75	.73	.53	.65	.88	.70	.69	.60	.70	.75	.87	.71
Campesinado	.38	.57	.35	.35	.41	.58	.71	.42	.42	.42	.40	.30	.43	.62	.35	.46	.34	.61	.45	.58	.47
Urban Proletariat	.81	.54	.50	.50	.47	.64	.72	.49	.48	.47	.47	.31	.44	.69	.38	.58	.34	.66	.61	.69	.54
Military Establishment	.95	.98	.99	.98	.70	.35	.75	.88	.96	.90	.94	.86	.94	.62	.94	.97	.96	.98	.92	.69	.86
The Church	.60	.56	.54	.54	.76	.50	.24	.64	.71	.63	.64	.55	.62	.43	.61	.54	.65	.60	.46	.53	.57
Anti-Government Insurgents	.73	.40	.37	.37	.49	.25	.24	.38	.36	.61	.51	.31	.36	.43	.37	.33	.30	.35	.51	.35	.40
Power Rating Total	.70	.63	.64	.65	.67	.55	.49	.66	.66	.68	.69	.55	.64	.62	.64	.65	.60	.63	.65	.62	.63

39

Nicaragua, and Panama. The reverse was generally true in South America. Industrialists ranked higher than landed oligarchs or foreign interests in Argentina, Brazil, Chile, Colombia, Peru, and Venezuela. The scholarly image of the power of foreign interests in the Central American-Caribbean region appears to be a direct reflection of the historic pattern of U.S. military intervention in the hemisphere. One scholar lists sixty-three instances of overt military intervention in Latin America by the United States between 1800 and the advent of the Good Neighbor era of the 1930s, and of these fifty-three occurred in Central America or the Caribbean (including Mexico and Puerto Rico).[4] In some cases the military action was followed by years of occupation (e.g., Cuba, Haiti, Panama, and Puerto Rico). Two post-Good-Neighbor-Policy-era interventions can be cited, Guatemala in 1954 and the Dominican Republic in 1965. The frequent military action by the United States is usually explained as an early concern for hemispheric defense and later for U.S. business interests plus an ongoing concern for the Canal Zone in Panama. The growth of multinational corporations has perpetuated and perhaps even extended the dependency of Latin American countries on the United States (see Chapter Five) while providing a justification (or excuse) for more military interventions.

Table 5 suggests a general pattern in which the power of the elites adversely affects the power of the masses. Of particular note is the inverse relationship between the power of the landed oligarchy and that of the *campesinado* (-.67). This pattern is particularly strong in the agrarian states of Central America, i.e., El Salvador, Guatemala, Honduras, and Nicaragua, and the Caribbean, i.e., Dominican Republic and Haiti. In these states, all ranking in the lower half on the democracy index over the thirty year period, the peasant's access to decision-making in government is seen as being directly (and negatively) affected by entrenched landed interests. The power of the urban proletariat seems particularly usurped by a powerful landed oligarchy although there is a modest positive relationship between the power of the industrialists and the power of the urban proletariat. The reverse of the Central American-Caribbean pattern seems evident in the more industrialized states of South America. The modernizing, urbanized states of this region have generally been more democratic over the past thirty years (see Table 3), perhaps because the power of the various contenders has been more concentrated. We will return to this point below. The power of the Church, military, and foreign interests is inversely related to both the urban proletariat and the *campesinado*. These traditionally anti-democratic forces (anti-democratic because none can be held politically accountable to the people) predictably hinder effective political involvement by the masses.

The only positive relationships associated with strong military influence are those of foreign interests, the Church, and to a far lesser extent, landed oligarchy and anti-government insurgents. The generally positive association between anti-government forces and elite contenders is probably explained in part as a reaction by the masses' low accessibility to the political power of elite-dominated

FIGURE 2

THE SOCIAL AND ECONOMIC CORRELATES OF
POLITICAL DEMOCRACY AND SYSTEM STABILITY

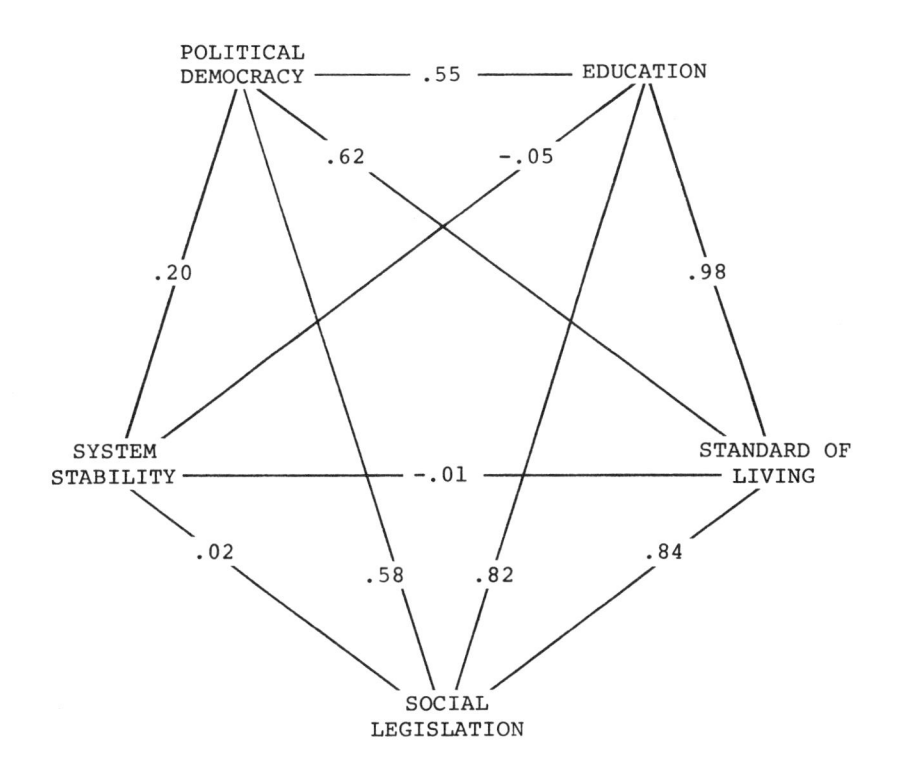

years, the relationship between the image of a commitment to social legislation and political stability is apparently understood by all.

POLITICAL DEMOCRACY: FOUR CASES

Various thirty-year patterns can be seen in Figure 3. The hemisphere's "most democratic" country (Costa Rica) and the "least democratic" (Paraguay) show remarkable consistency for the period while the only hemispheric country to have experienced a Marxist revolution (Cuba) and a country claiming a military-directed revolution (Peru) have had a more erratic pattern.

Costa Rica and Paraguay, the "most democratic" and the "least democratic" countries in Latin America respectively according to the general scholarly image are also the first and second least changing political systems in the hemisphere (see Table 3). While Costa Rica would appear to be strongly committed to democratic institutions (as were Uruguay and Chile), it was one of but four countries—Colombia, the Dominican Republic and Venezuela being the other three—in which the DRC in 1975 was higher than the Social Legislation rating. This is explained in part by the exceptionally high DRC in Costa Rica's case, but virtually all of Latin America has seen it necessary to place increased emphasis on major reform, particularly in light of Castro's success in Cuba and the model that country might suggest to dissidents everywhere. In this sense Cuba and Peru do not represent the exceptions to a Latin American pattern, but rather Costa Rica, along with Colombia, Venezuela and the Dominican Republic, do. The argument made by both Cuba and Peru, albeit from differing ideological perspectives, is that political democracy has deterred rather than facilitated fundamental change. Indeed in both cases there has been an inverse relationship between social legislation and political democracy.

In most respects Cuba and Peru offer sharp contrasts. Cuba has always been among the more "developed" countries in the hemisphere although politically it has been extremely volatile. The decline in Cuban democracy preceded the revolution and has generally continued beyond it. In the Peruvian case political democracy was not on the decline at the time of the military reformist government takeover in 1968, at least not in the collective eyes of scholars. On the other hand, socioeconomic progress did not result from the resurgence of democracy in the late fifties and sixties. What did occur, at least from the military perspective, was the emergence of a violent revolutionary threat from the left. It was this as much as anything that precipitated the military intervention. *What the two countries do share, however, is evidence that political democracy is neither a precondition for socioeconomic change nor necessarily a logical consequence of it.*

SUMMARY AND CONCLUSION

The scholarly image surveys suggest that democracy in Latin America is ephemeral at best and possibly even self-destructive as was Macondo. Figure 2 illustrates the basic dilemma in that democracy is at once associated with socio-

FIGURE 3

COMPARATIVE DEMOCRATIC RATING COEFFICIENTS: FOUR CASES

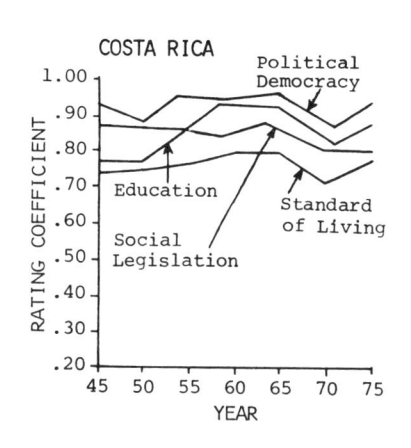

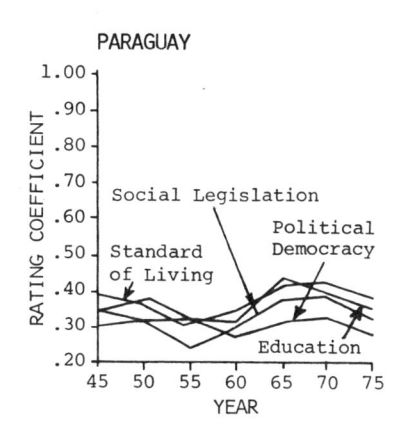

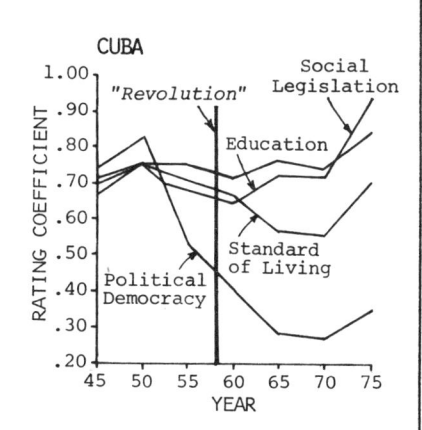

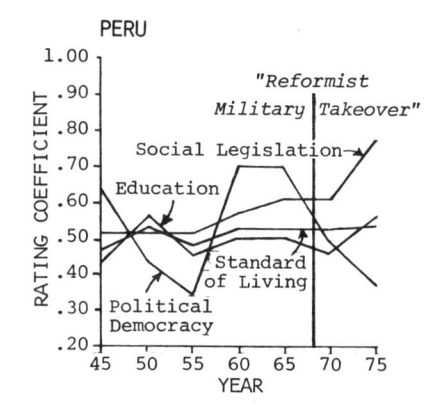

economic development and, simultaneously, political uncertainty or instability. Carried to its full extension this might imply that as a society moves toward the goals of socioeconomic development and political democracy, success therein becomes a source of new problems. One might reasonably ask: Can democracy survive in a society beset by social and economic inequities when priorities must be established and policies carried out to alleviate those inequities? The question, of course, is familiar. Successful democracy is by its very nature associated with an articulate public (possibly presupposing a reasonably high education level) having a strong sense of political efficacy and demanding accountability from its officials.

The constant threat of a sudden, total change of political power, when coupled with the extraordinary difficulty of changing objective social and economic conditions, will always create a greater challenge for political democracies based on citizen input and governmental accountability than for authoritarian regimes where power is concentrated. In a political democracy social reform may be a response to citizen demand and citizen scrutiny, whereas in the authoritarian system a reallocation of resources can be accomplished by strictly enforced demands for public sacrifice (e.g., Peru and possibly Brazil). Thus the authoritarian approach may have substantial appeal to two types of power contenders: one, those with a fundamental concern for maintaining the status quo, e.g., Paraguay, Haiti, and Nicaragua; and two, those with an interest in controlled development, e.g., Cuba and Peru. The former type may not result in much social or economic change, but neither does it face an immediate risk of overthrow. The latter type may or may not produce significant development, but the regime's vulnerability to political upheaval is minimized. Political democracies attempting to embark on programs of rapid socioeconomic reform face the worst of both worlds. On the one hand change is likely to be slow in coming, particularly since competing interests may fundamentally disagree on the goals as well as the methods, and on the other hand, the regime's vulnerability may be increased by the very effort of reform itself.

García Márquez's Macondo may have exhibited some of the trappings of democracy and the illusion of economic progress with the introduction of foreign investment. Eventually, however, the central government's commitment to democracy was subordinated to the concern for stability and to economic gains in Macondo, and its exposure to "modernization efforts" led to the village's demise. It can reasonably be argued that García Márquez's literary creation represents an accurate if hypothetical microcosm of Latin American societies. Both Chile and Uruguay, for example, expressed commitments to the ideal of political democracy and socioeconomic equality, and both countries suffered political upheaval and the imposition of authoritarian government. Paraguay, on the other hand, has the lowest democratic image in the hemisphere but also the second least political change over the thirty-year period from 1945 to 1975.

It was noted that Anderson's model of the Latin American political process emphasized the power capabilities available to the relevant power contenders in society.

TABLE 5

THE INTERRELATIONSHIP BETWEEN THE POWER OF
POLITICAL CONTENDERS IN LATIN AMERICA

	Landed Oligarchy	Industrialists	Church	Military	Foreign Interests	Anti-Gov't Insur.	Urban Proletariat	Campesinado
Landed Oligarchy	.00	.72	.09	.64	.27	-.79	-.67	
Industrialists		-.04	-.09	-.33	.58	.28	.02	
Church			.25	-.32	.26	-.55	-.48	
Military				.25	.10	-.24	-.40	
Foreign Interests					-.01	-.71	-.46	
Anti-Gov't Insur.						.04	-.16	
Urban Proletariat							.73	
Campesinado								

governments. Still, the Argentine and Uruguayan cases of insurgency during the 1960s and 1970s may challenge such an assertion.

The scholarly image of "traditional elites" (i.e., Church, foreign interests, industrialists, landed oligarchy, and military) possessing strong power capabilities is a reflection of the literature which continues to stress the power of elites in Latin American society. This alone is not sufficient to disqualify polities from wearing the democratic label, however, except as an "ideal type." The pluralist model of democracy (polyarchy) does not require equality of influence but rather a diffusion of power among several competing elites. Dahl comments as follows:

> If there is anything to be said for the processes that actually distinguish democracy (polyarchy) from dictatorship, it is not discoverable in the clear-cut distinction between government by a minority and government by minorities. As compared with the political processes of a dictatorship, the characteristics of polyarchy greatly extend the number, size, and diversity of the minorities whose preferences will influence the outcome of governmental decisions.[5]

In short, the question is not whether minorities have great influence but which minorities, and to what extent the power and influence are concentrated with the very few.

A strong direct role for the military, foreign interests and the Church is probably a detriment to the cause of democracy as neither can be readily held accountable except through successful armed confrontation or expropriation, this given the general absence of rule-of-law in most of Latin America. Therefore, to the extent to which any of these contenders is able to exert substantial power in political decisions affecting society, the democratic process is encumbered or even invalidated. On the other hand, a powerful role for industrialists and the landed oligarchy is not necessarily *ipso facto* an impediment to democracy. If some contenders have the capacity to counterbalance others, pluralist democracy or polyarchy can remain intact, but this is rare in Latin America during the 1970s.

Several related hypotheses about power and democracy were formulated for the purpose of drawing inferences about the utility of the five measures of political democracy in the Fitzgibbon-Johnson Index as possible components of a pluralist model.

H_1 : *Political democracy is negatively correlated with the national power ranking of the military establishment.*

Following the line of reasoning developed above, the assumption is that the military's non-accountability in most of Latin America is incompatible with democracy. Therefore we would expect to find a strong inverse relationship between country rankings on democracy (DRC) and country rankings of the military's power (PRC).

H_2 : *Political democracy is negatively correlated with the national power ranking of foreign interests.*

Again, the question of accountability is critical. The dependency thesis outlined in Chapter Five asserts that foreign domination usually renders democratic processes impotent.

H_3 : *Political democracy is negatively correlated with the national power rankings of "traditional elites."*

The "traditional elites" included in this analysis were the military, landed oligarchy, industrialists, the Church, and foreign interests. Computing a combined PRC by aggregating scores of each of the five power contenders within each country, the twenty polities were then ranked and correlated with democratic ratings (DRCs). Even though traditional elites may exercise considerable power and still be considered democratic by pluralist criteria, it is probably less likely that democracy will flourish where elites approach omnipotence. It was for this reason that another hypothesis was formulated.

H_4 : *Political democracy is negatively correlated with the concentration of power in the hands of a single power-contending group.*

This hypothesis directly reflects on Dahl's formulation of polyarchy noted above; i.e., the question is not whether a majority or a minority has the greatest influence but rather whether influence is sufficiently dispersed among minorities (assumed to be the more influential) to insure representation for competing interests. For purposes of this analysis, *concentration of power in the hands of a single group is determined by calculating a ratio of the power rating of the most powerful of seven contending interests in each country to the summation of power rating coefficients of all other relevant contenders* (the single group referred to will usually be the military and we should also clarify that anti-government insurgents were not included in this theoretic formulation as they are not normally a part of the ostensibly democratic process). The resulting measure, basically a variation ratio (V.R.), provides a basis for ranking countries according to the concentration-dispersion of power. A Spearman's rho is then computed. The formula for variation ratio is as follows: $V.R. = 1 - \frac{fm}{n}$, where fm = frequency of the modal class (modal class here being interpreted as the score for the power contender with the highest PRC), and n = number of observations (for our purposes the summation of PRCs for the seven relevant contenders). The military was rated the most powerful in all but five countries. Industrialists were seen as being the most powerful in Colombia, Mexico, and Venezuela; the landed oligarchy in Nicaragua; and foreign interests in Costa Rica. In these cases industrialists, landed oligarchy, and foreign interests were used to represent the modal class.

H_5 : *Political democracy is positively correlated with the national power rankings of mass-based groups.*

The "mass-based" groups included in this analysis were the *campesinado* and the urban proletariat. Once again, anti-government insurgents are probably inappropriate for consideration as a measure of democracy. The underlying assumption of the above hypothesis is simply that the greater the power of contenders representing large numbers of people, the greater will be the competition in the decision-making process.

The following Spearman's rhos were found for the relationship between democracy and power of the various contenders:

H_1 : *Military*   -.63 *(significant at .01)*

H_2 : *Foreign Interests*   -.40 *(significant at .05)*

H_3 : *Traditional Elites:*   -.21 *(not significant)*

H_4: Concentration
in Single Group: $-.85$ (significant at .01)

H_5: Mass-Based
Groups: $+.65$ (significant at .01)

    The correlations were computed for the 1975 five-item index of democracy and the power index also constructed in 1975. Correlations between the original fifteen-item index and the power index were not used as the resulting coefficients produce artificially high r values. This is because of the item duplication between the fifteen-item index and the power index. For example "absence of foreign domination" and the power of "foreign interests," "absence of ecclesiastical controls" and the power of the "Church," "civilian supremacy over the military establishment" and the power of the military overlap and tend to be partial reflections of the same phenomena, albeit for different indices, thereby greatly increasing the value of the correlation coefficient. The same problem is present with the five-item index although to a lesser extent. Here we find that civilian supremacy and the power of the military are but two sides of the same coin, and an interpretation of the correlation coefficient should be made with this in mind.

    The data support all but the third hypothesis. No statistically significant relationship was found to exist between the power of "traditional elites" and democracy in Latin America. A careful examination of the data indicates that five of the eight power contenders were "traditional elites" and that only in five countries (Argentina, Costa Rica, Cuba, Mexico, and Peru) did more than one non-elite group rank in the top five interest groups surveyed. In all probability the power of traditional elites was seen as being so all-pervasive throughout Latin America that meaningful distinctions are not possible, albeit the overall level of democracy in the hemisphere in 1975 was extremely low, suggesting that the power of the elites does detract from democracy.

    We found a statistically significant relationship, $-.63$, between the power of the military and democracy. This tends to be inflated by the inclusion of "civilian supremacy" in the five-item index, as noted above. Nevertheless, the virtual omnipotence of the military throughout much of Latin America was surely seen by the panel of experts as being detrimental to the democratic cause. This is partially confirmed by the overall decline of the hemisphere's cumulative DRCs since 1960, a period that corresponds closely to a notable increase in the number of military regimes.

    Both the relationships between democracy and the power of foreign interests and between democracy and mass-based groups were found to be significant. The moderate negative correlation between foreign interests and democracy was not unexpected although Costa Rica, the country with the highest democratic rating coefficient in 1975 was the only country in which foreign interests rated the highest of the eight power contenders within the country. This apparent contradiction may be explained in part by the fact that in Costa Rica, where officially no military exists, competition for power occurs almost exclusively between civilians (and foreigners), and even foreign interests are not dominant. The range in power rating coefficients, excluding military and anti-government insurgents, neither of which are important forces in Costa Rica, was narrower than in any other country in Latin America. This indicates a comparatively high level of competition between power contenders within that nation.

Looking at Table 6, the strong positive correlation between democracy and mass-based contenders was also consistent with the pluralist model. The power of traditional elites throughout most of Latin America can be considered almost a "given," but in those societies where mass-based contenders can emerge as significant political forces, representation for a broad spectrum of the population is possible. This is confirmed further by the moderate positive associations between democracy and both the urban proletariat and the *campesinado* when considered individually.

TABLE 6

POWER, DEMOCRACY, AND STABILITY IN LATIN AMERICA

	Democracy	System Stability	Power Concentration
Landed Oligarchy	-.17	.38	-.03
Industrialists	.50	-.06	-.38
Church	-.09	.30	-.06
Military	-.03	-.23	.64
Foreign Interests	-.40	-.01	.20
Urban Proletariat	.37	-.34	-.48
Campesinado	.42	-.03	-.31
Anti-Gov't Insur.	.30	.03	-.30
Traditional Elites	-.21	.11	.02
Masses	.65	-.15	-.49
Democracy - 1975		-.11	-.85
System Stability			.01
Power Concentration			

Perhaps the most important of the five hypotheses was the fourth, suggesting a negative relationship between democracy and a concentration of power with a single power contender (regardless of which contender). Again the hypothesis is firmly rooted in the pluralist model. A -.85 correlation was found, suggesting a strong pluralist basis for the democratic rating system of the five-item index of democracy as interpreted by the panel of scholars.

SUMMARY

The growth of democracy is often said to depend on a modernizing state, particularly one characterized by industrialization and an emerging middle class.[6] Aggregating the responses of our panel of scholars certainly suggests that such a belief is widely held. Those countries which have progressed the most in the development of a modern economy seem also to be those that rank highest on the democratic scale.

Yet democracy is not necessarily equated with stability as noted earlier. Indeed, social and economic change may be antipathetic to the forces for democracy at least in the short run. Whether this is the result of an entrenched elite perceiving its interests threatened by change or the relative deprivation of the masses, or a combination of the two, the road to modernization within the democratic context is difficult.

Once again, many Latin American societies seem to be playing out the drama of Macondo. Democracy and economic modernization seem pitted against one another, and the forces for democracy are engulfed by some modernization efforts. Democracy, or at least the illusion of democracy, is sacrificed when a diffusion of power among elite and non-elite contenders alike would seem to threaten (in the eyes of those with readily available capabilities to control the situation) a privileged socioeconomic order generally fashioned by the few over the years. Like Macondo where elections are accepted only to the extent that they confirm the vision held by the elites, democracy in Latin America is frequently contingent on the willingness of the masses to ratify that model of development designed and implemented by the traditional forces in society. Quality of life for the masses usually suffers, as in the novelist's vision. And that suggests a distinction between *social* and *political* democracy, an issue to which we turn in the final chapter. But first we treat an external force that may condition the entire range of democratic expressions in Latin America, i.e., foreign interventionism.

FOOTNOTES - CHAPTER FOUR

1. Charles Anderson, *Politics and Economic Change in Latin America* (Princeton: D. Van Nostrand, 1967), p. 89.

2. Robert A. Dahl, *A Preface to Democratic Theory*, Phoenix Books (Chicago: University of Chicago Press, 1963), p. 9.

3. New York Times News Service, "Latin Military Regimes Repel Leftist Assault," *The San Diego Union*, August 1, 1976, p. C-7.

4. Herbert K. Tillema, *Appeal to Force: American Military Intervention in an Era of Containment* (New York: Thomas Y. Crowell, 1973), pp. 218-225.

5. Dahl, *A Preface to Democratic Theory*, p. 133.

6. Some scholars have viewed the middle class in Latin America as a dangerous myth *vis-à-vis* both democracy and stability. This is the argument of Sven Lindquist, *The Shadow: Latin America Faces the Seventies* (New York: Penguin Books, 1972), esp. pp. 52-53. He argues that middle class governments are occasionally swept into power by the discontented masses who have been promised great reforms, that there is no apparatus in the political system for making good on this promise given the power structure, that the middle-class governments then indebt themselves to the United States foreign assistance programs as a defense against the upper classes and to try to deliver on past promises. Inflation ensues and hurts the workers who begin disturbances leading to instability and violence out of which class dictatorship and/or military-elite dictatorship emerges. This is not unlike the spectre of Macondo, and it is directly relevant to the considerations raised about U.S. foreign interventionism in the chapter to follow.

CHAPTER FIVE
POWER, DEMOCRACY AND DEPENDENCY
THE HEMISPHERIC PICTURE OF INTERVENTION

From the preceding chapter it can be seen that a strong *negative* correlation exists (at least in the minds of our experts) between military power and political democracy. It is hard to overlook the complicity of United States foreign assistance policy in this equation. Any assistance to dictatorial regimes, be it economic or military aid, serves to release local funds with which to finance a tyrant's hold on his people. There are cases in which a given military establishment might have rebelled against a dictator and removed him had it not been for United States support, a speculation which, of course, does not mean that a more human rights oriented government would be established. But there is reason to believe that without the support of the United States such regimes as the Somoza dynasty in Nicaragua would have toppled long ago. The Nicaraguan dictator, "Tachito" Somoza, suffered a heart attack during 1977 and late that year there was open speculation about members of his own *guardia* planning to oust him and of members of the upper classes openly sympathizing with, in some cases even joining, the *sandinista* guerrillas. Scholars of Nicaragua have noted the potential within the military for opposing the dictatorship of which some militarists have been a part (Richard Millett's excellent work *Guardians of the Dynasty,* 1977, being a good example) were it not for support from the United States.

United States aid is not a recent phenomenon in Latin America. Since the early 1950s when Raúl Prebisch's scheme of development and of foreign assistance for development enjoyed prestige, the hemisphere has witnessed a Marxist revolution in Cuba, an attempted socialist revolution in Chile, and a drive in several countries (Mexico and Brazil being among the most prominent examples) toward massive industrialization based upon aid from the "more developed" nations of the world. In practice this most often meant American aid although significant inputs were made by Canadian, Japanese, and West German interests. But again there is abundant testimony to the effect that not all of the aid ended up in socioeconomic development and labor-intensive industries. Much of it, apparently, made it possible even indirectly for dictatorial regimes to prosper. The so-called "Brazilian miracle" has meant that the Brazilian people are poorer in the absolute sense than they were before the military overthrow of a popular and constitutional government in 1964, a coup in which it is now known the United States government had some complicity. There have been no Argentine or Mexican miracles; there citizen purchasing power has dropped as much as forty percent during recent years in both countries. Along with this have come political authoritarianism and repressive violations of human rights. The socioeconomic-political situation in Chile is so notorious as of this writing that it hardly needs further commentary.

An overall balance sheet on the Prebisch thesis (massive industrialization via massive foreign aid complemented by policies of import substitution to reduce trade deficits and control inflation) has failed to produce significant economic progress anywhere in the hemisphere. It seems to have been accompanied by increased United States intervention, both economic and political-military, in the affairs of Latin American states. The ill-fated ALPRO (Alliance for Progress) seemed to be an ultimate expression of the Prebisch thesis in the minds of many observers. Perhaps Teotonio dos Santos best described the position of leading social scientists in Latin America with respect to the obstacles to development when he offered his definition of dependency. "Dependency," he asserted:

> is a situation in which a certain group of countries have their economies conditioned by the growth and expansion of other economies. The relation of interdependence between two or more economies, and between these and world trade, assumes the form of dependency when some countries (the dominant ones) can only reflect that expansion, and this can have either a positive or negative effect on its immediate development. In all cases, the basic situation of dependency is conducive to a global situation in which the dependent countries remain behind and under the exploitation of the dominant countries.[1]

Dependency theorists in Latin America argue that it is imperative that the nature of dependency be understood if applicable models of development are to emerge and be implemented. In the past, they argue, Latin America has merely aped the United States and Western European models of capitalistic development. Accordingly the first step toward devising a new strategy is to end the condition of dependency which has molded Latin America and convert it into a form more useful to development as in Europe and the United States. Those who adhere to the dependency thesis tend to reject the Prebisch model, programs like the Alliance for Progress, and the supporting foreign policies that draw Latin America into the ideological war being directed by the world's super powers.

In this chapter we will examine briefly some political antecedents of Latin American dependency, the impact of the Alliance for Progress and the scholarly image of power and democracy in Latin America. Our purpose is to show that U.S. aid policy has been associated with the decline of democracy rather than economic development within a democratic framework, just as foreign economic intervention hastened the demise of Macondo in our literary-based model.

ANTECEDENTS

The shadow of North American influence has been cast over Latin America in many ways: diplomatic, military, social-touristic, and through what is called economic development aid. All of this has meant a variety of interventions that have at times pleased the "host" peoples of Latin America; but more often than not they have been displeased. We will take up salient aspects of the various interventions in this chapter. A United States Senate study issued in 1973 admits that the United States might be couching its development aid to the LDC's (less developed countries) in a context deliberately intended to force these countries to spend that aid on North American products. It also notes that despite the diplomatic leverage which development assistance is supposed to give the United States over the Third World these nations frequently vote anti-American in the United Nations--a great embarrassment to the aid givers.[2] What is the rationale for the United States policy of giving its money (which many feel is desperately needed at home) to assist the development of foreign nations?

A relatively conservative statement of the rationale is provided by James W. Howe who says that "helping development" is based on four fundamental long range propositions. The first is that of international cooperation under the assumption that most local problems will have some international ramifications. The second, a corollary of the first, is that nations that are achieving their goals will be more likely to cooperate in the international community of nations and not become sources of conflict. Third, he suggests that development aid can solve humanitarian and other domestic problems and this can be defended on a moral basis. And lastly, he argues that if the increasing disparity between the rich and poor is not arrested, the consequences for Planet Earth in the year 2000 will probably be disastrous.[3] This, we repeat, is the statement of a relatively conservative author who, with caveats, supports some form of continuing U.S. aid to the Third World. Yet the same author also admits that the giving and the withholding of aid may be a form of interventionist imperialism, or at least it may be widely seen as such as in the case of Chile in 1973.

Let us consider the more obvious forms of intervention, e.g., use of armed force. A chronology of U.S. military interventions in Latin America between 1798 and 1945 reflects scores of major incidents, each composed of dozens of minor conflicts, culminating in the threat of military force which helped defeat the Sandino guerrilla uprising in Nicaragua during the late 1920s.[4] Throughout this period the United States acted under the Monroe Doctrine, declared in 1823, which stated in effect that the western hemisphere would be our protectorate and sphere of influence *vis-à-vis* outside powers.[5] This was later bolstered by the so-called Roosevelt Corollary which Theodore Roosevelt devised as a justification of his Big Stick police policy in the Caribbean, particularly around the turn of the century when European nations threatened to intervene in Latin America to collect debts. In addition Roosevelt engineered the seizure of the province of

Panama from Colombia in 1903 so as to allow the United States to build the present canal under a perpetual lease of land. Thus, under the Big Stick policy a tiny nation, Panama, was created by force and proclaimed in flagrant violation of international law but to the advantage of United States interests.

Similar views guided our actions in such nations as the Dominican Republic, Haiti, Nicaragua and Honduras, all of which were occupied by U.S. forces at one time or another during the twentieth century as customs receiverships were established to guarantee payment of debts and prevent European interventions.

One can readily understand the historical legacy of resentment that built up in Latin America against the Yankee shadow during the major part of two centuries. The anti-fascism of the 1940s was replaced in the United States by an intense and often hysterical anti-communism in the 1950s. This national mood was molded in large part by the witch hunts of Senator Joseph McCarthy and by the Dulles brothers, John Foster and Allen (Secretary of State and Director of the CIA, respectively). The Dulles brothers, fanatically anti-communist and preaching "better dead than red," were also (incidentally) one-time partners in a law firm that represented the United Fruit Company in its international dealings. That company during the early 1950s was the target for a nationalization campaign in Guatemala by the leftist government of Jacobo Arbenz Guzmán. In addition to taking over company lands the Arbenz regime revealed that the United Fruit Company owned a railroad (IRCA) which charged the highest rates in the world and had not paid any taxes to the government of Guatemala since its incorporation half a century earlier.[6] Arbenz also threatened the United States (that is, in the eyes of the Dulles brothers) by purchasing arms from the Iron Curtain countries. So the brothers Dulles decided to invade Guatemala.

In 1961, with Guatemala firmly in the grip of a pro-U.S. dictatorship, that nation's lands were used to prepare for an invasion of Cuba also financed by the CIA and intended to topple the Communist regime of Fidel Castro. This debacle failed due to U.S. mismanagement and to the surprising resistance of the Cuban revolutionary society.

But fear of another Cuba prevailed in Washington. President Lyndon Johnson had also inherited some of the "red menace" mentality from John Foster Dulles (and, frankly, from Kennedy). Across a short waterway from Cuba lay Haiti and the Dominican Republic, the latter having had its capital city, Santo Domingo, defiantly renamed Trujillo City by the family dictatorship that had prevailed with U.S. assistance since the late 1920s. But in 1961, suddenly the dictator was dead and the following year elections were held under supervision of the Organization of American States.

In Trujillo's place came Juan Bosch, a leftist intellectual who was elected democratically. He assumed power in February of 1963 but proved to be too leftist to please U.S. Ambassador John Bartlow Martin. Bosch felt that Martin was forcing him to revert to the Trujillo style of imprisoning, deporting, or killing anyone suspected of being a Communist,[7] and the State Department soon felt that the Bosch government was drifting toward fraternity with Cuba. Communists, it was feared, were being allowed too great a role in the Dominican government's affairs. So in September of the same year in which he took office Bosch was deposed and exiled by his military. The U.S. Government smiled approval as a provisional government was formed under Donald Reid Cabral, himself reputed to be a CIA agent.[8]

But by April of 1965 the Reid regime was in trouble. Constitutionalist forces wanted to return Bosch to his lawful presidency. The military had contrary ambitions of its own. Consequently when the constitutionalists sought to unseat Reid (and they did), the military used its guns and assumed power. The preponderance of the evidence is that the United States did nothing to help the Reid Cabral government. It also opposed the constitutionalists and gave support to the right-wing military which probably would have been defeated had the U.S. not intervened. But the U.S. did intervene and massively with over 20,000 soldiers and marines. It later brought in troops from several other Latin American countries to give the impression that an "Inter-American Peace Force" had been created.

The Dominican Republic was a relatively easy place for the U.S. to intervene, to create an "Inter-American Peace Force" as a legitimizing tactic and then withdraw once the threat of a "second Cuba" had passed.[9] The Dominican Republic was politically weak and tied economically to the United States to such an extent that an invasion could be justified to the American people in 1965. However the political costs to the U.S. since then in hemispheric prestige have been staggering and can only be gauged by such trends as the gradual reestablishment of relations with Cuba by most of the OAS nations during the 1970s and the discrediting of the U.S. "red menace" mentality that lingered on after the Dulles brothers period.

THE ALPRO SYNDROME

According to Gerassi's analysis[10] the terms of Alliance for Progress financing were such as to effectively preclude land reform, even though much lip service was given to this principle. The U.S. forbade its "beneficiaries" from buying goods with their Alliance for Progress loans in other countries, such as those in Europe where the goods might be cheaper. All funds had to be spent in a "member country" of the Alliance.[11] In practice this almost always meant the United States. Although much noise was made in public about the "loans" which were granted to the recipient countries, in reality few true loans were made. The countries got a credit in the United States instead. The United States played a role of banker and mercantilist at once, granting credits and then saying, "Spend it only at our store." This inevitably meant that when the credit ("loan") was used the recipient country suffered a dollar drain for it had to pay money into Washington. This was of course favorable to the economy of the United States. When funds were given as outright grants to the countries they were frequently in the form of budget support agreements in which the United States asked few questions about why a government could not meet its payroll and thereby kept the country's administrative apparatus "hooked" through indebtedness.

This in turn made it easier for the State Department to "turn the screws" on Latin American governments to force them to grant concessions to American companies.[12]

But the specific promises of the Alliance, i.e., raising of the per capita income of each Latin American country by 2.5 percent a year, elimination of illiteracy by 1970, sweeping developments in low-cost housing, and all the rest, were not honored anywhere among the ALPRO nations. Many of them were achieved in Cuba which got no ALPRO funds. This contributed to the growth of anti-American sentiment throughout the hemisphere. Marxism came to be seen as a feasible out, the ALPRO seemed to have cheated the people. Only Cuba had eliminated its illiteracy and all Latin America was watching the progress of the Cuban Revolution. The democratic victory of Marxist Salvador Allende in the Chilean presidential election of 1970 was a final unwelcome fruit of the generous ALPRO investment in that country over nearly a decade.

What American foreign policy pretended to achieve in Latin America during the decade of the 1960s was the creation of socioeconomic conditions in which a non-violent democratic politics could flourish, i.e., the opposite of Macondo. What resulted instead was reinforcement of the military elites and wealthy oligarchies who ruled most of Latin America at the beginning of the decade. This was accomplished through an ingeniously complicated system of indirect subsidies for North American firms who contracted for ALPRO money to be spent in Latin America, through an increased subsidization of the already heavily subsidized American farmer (the Public Law 480 program) and by direct loans and grants to Latin American governments.

If the ultimate goal of the Alliance was the achievement of political democracy, or at least the conditions for its nurture, then on balance the result is shocking. The Alliance was proclaimed in 1961 when such important nations as Argentina, Bolivia, Brazil, Chile, Guatemala, Panama, Peru, and Uruguay enjoyed popularly elected governments. By 1977 all of these were subjected to authoritarian military rule, in most cases merciless tyrannies. Most of them still received some form of United States aid and most of their soldiers still used American-made weapons to suppress the local population. By 1977 only Colombia and Venezuela had even the appearance of constitutional government in the Latin part of South America; in the remainder of Latin America, Costa Rica had the only truly free popular government. In 1977 the new Carter administration began an active campaign to cut aid to countries whose governments violated human rights. It is too soon to assess the impact of this new U.S. aid policy.

Most of the billions of dollars that the United States invested in Latin America during the 1960s was channeled through civilian structures like USAID, the International Development Bank, etc., and it was this civilian image that the Department of State preferred to foster. But other aid went through military, CIA and various classified channels which the public was not permitted to know about in the interest of "security concerns." It is an educated guess that the figure for such "classified aid" is substantially in excess of the figures the American people were told about officially.

Not only were Latin Americans placed under a reinforced debt peonage by the ALPRO, but to make it worse the North American taxpayer was expected to pick up the bill. President Kennedy did not say this in so many words at Punta del Este. Yet the United States taxpayers would be held liable for the risks that American commercial interests would take in Latin America, risks that such investors would normally be expected to assume for themselves. Bureaucrats, informally in league with potential investors, erected multilateral aid schemes to safeguard the flow of money to Latin America free from the surveillance of the United States Congress.[13] This was a sort of "welfare imperialism."

Latin American economies have resembled the "remora association" in which a sucker fish attaches itself to a bigger fish and lives from the dribblings which fall from the larger fish's mouth.[14] Into this relationship, unhealthy for either party, the Alliance for Progress entered, floundered, and reinforced the "remoras," the uncompetitive affluent class of local mercantilists and small industrialists who sold dearly at home while hiding all the while behind protective tariffs. The affluence of this class of Alliance beneficiaries increased as did the gap between rich and poor. The blindness of Alliance for Progress officials (or their cunning) allowed this parasitic mendicancy to flourish. Significantly of course, gross investment as a percentage of gross national product declined during the Alliance years, but the flow of U.S. dollars continued despite the nature of the performance. It seemed as if keeping the AID bureaucracy going was the principal motive behind the continued outpouring of largesse. AID did its best to hide its record of failure and almost concealed an average of some 300 million dollars per year in unauthorized aid that was being doled out in addition to the one billion per year committed under the Alliance.[15]

At some point these economics of failure had to stop, and at that point President Nixon ended (at least in name) the Alliance for Progress in 1972. From then on it was to be Action for Progress and "low profile." As of this writing in 1977 it is premature to characterize the Carter administration's approach to assisting the nations of Latin America. His most dramatic change, as noted earlier, has been to use withdrawal of aid (or the threat thereof) as part of a worldwide human rights crusade, one that has been somewhat inconsistent where certain key nations were concerned; e.g., he has been vocal against Chile and silent on Mexico.

THE IMPACT OF U.S. AID ON LATIN AMERICAN DEMOCRACY

The record of U.S. aid and hemispheric intervention, as confirmed by the 1973 Senate report, is in contradiction to the stated objectives of economic development within strong democratic processes. In light of the economic stagnation and precipitous decline of democracy in Latin America, one might well ask what rationale, if any, was used in the allocation of aid. Dependency theorists usually argue that aid is used as a calculated weapon to dominate the region both politically and economically. The preceding discussion certainly suggests that aid is in fact a form of intervention and one that may be accomplished while ostensibly maintaining a low profile policy image. Selective aid and a low profile policy was followed by Secretary of State Henry Kissinger's invitation to Latin American foreign ministers to join the U.S. in the establishment of a "new dialog." The more cynical might observe that the invitation came on October 5, 1973, less than two weeks after the Marxist president of Chile, Salvador Allende, was overthrown and assassinated in circumstances that at least indirectly involved the United States government.

Former U.S. Ambassador to the Organization of American States, Sol Linowitz, recently chaired a Commission on U.S.-Latin American Relations whose report called for a fundamental change in U.S. policy toward the region. Coming on the eve of President Carter's inauguration, the prestigious commission, which included Secretary of the Treasury W. Michael Blumenthal, acknowledged the negative impact U.S. intervention has had on democracy and human rights in the hemisphere.

Our own data seem to support the contention that U.S. aid has not been used to build democratic institutions, nor has it in fact had that effect. Table 7 shows how aid was distributed to Latin America for the 1962-1974 period, roughly the time frame of the ALPRO. The five largest recipients of aid during that period were, in order: Brazil, Colombia, Chile, Dominican Republic, and Bolivia. Of the five only Colombia and the Dominican Republic are presently governed by civilian regimes, and in the Dominican Republic, Balaguer came to power as a consequence of the previously discussed U.S. military intervention in 1965.

If indeed the U.S. aid program was designed to build and solidify democratic institutions in Latin America, the program cannot be considered too successful. As Table 9 indicates, the relationship between U.S. aid in the 1962-1974 period and democracy for a comparable period (computed mean democratic rating for 1965, 1970, and 1975) was modest.

According to the 1975 image index of political democracy the five largest recipients ranked 16th, 3rd, 18th, 6th, and 15th, respectively, on the democratic scale. On the basis of total per capita assistance received, Panama, the Dominican Republic, Bolivia, Chile, and Nicaragua were the top recipients, ranking 11th, 6th, 15th, 18th, and 17th, respectively, on the 1975 democratic index. From Table 9 it can be seen that the relationship between U.S. assistance and democracy is presented in a more favorable light when total dollar figures are used rather than per capita assistance. The per capita figures tend to place greater emphasis on the smaller, less populated countries of Central America--countries that have traditionally ranked low on the democratic index (see Table 1). For example, the Dominican Republic, El Salvador, Guatemala, Honduras, Nicaragua, and Panama ranked 2nd, 12th, 13th, 10th, 5th, and 1st, respectively, in per capita aid received, but only 4th, 15th, 11th, 17th, 12th and 10th in dollar totals.

All six countries ranked in the bottom half of the mean democratic ranking over the thirty-year period (see Table 3). Conversely, the larger nations of South America generally received larger sums of money and other forms of

TABLE 7

UNITED STATES ECONOMIC AND MILITARY ASSISTANCE TO LATIN AMERICA 1962-1974*

	Economic Aid	Rank	Military Aid	Rank	Total	Rank	% Paid Back	Rank	Population Estimates
Argentina	186.1	9	194.3	2	380.4	7	44	1	25.3
Bolivia	446.2	5	42.5	7	488.7	5	6	18	5.0
Brazil	2,197.0	1	312.0	1	2,509.4	1	9	12.3	101.3
Chile	799.0	3	152.6	3	951.6	3	12	8	10.4
Colombia	1,256.8	2	101.7	5	1,424.7	2	11	9.5	23.7
Costa Rica	146.4	14	1.7	18	148.1	16	7	15.3	2.0
Cuba	-0-	20	-0-	20	-0-	20	0	20	8.9
Dominican Rep.	508.9	4	27.2	11	536.1	4	9	12.3	4.8
Ecuador	251.8	8	36.4	9	288.2	9	20	3	6.7
El Salvador	145.1	15	8.8	16	153.9	15	9	12.3	3.8
Guatemala	176.3	11	30.4	10	206.7	11	7	15.3	5.6
Haiti	64.2	19	0.7	19	64.9	19	2	19	5.6
Honduras	130.2	16	9.7	15	139.9	17	10	11	3.0
Mexico	151.4	13	10.5	14	161.9	14	17	4.5	56.2
Nicaragua	171.8	12	16.0	13	187.8	12	7	15.3	2.2
Panama	268.0	7	6.9	17	274.9	10	11	9.5	1.6
Paraguay	112.2	18	17.9	12	130.1	18	17	4.5	2.7
Peru	346.4	6	94.9	6	441.3	6	14	7	14.9
Uruguay	146.7	17	40.1	8	163.1	13	16	6	3.0
Venezuela	182.5	10	110.0	4	292.5	8	32	2	11.9

*Sources: *U.S. Overseas Loans and Grants* (Obligations and Authorizations July 1, 1945 to June 30, 1975) (Washington: Agency for International Development. Published once a year.

1973 World Population Data Sheet (Washington, D.C.: Population Reference Bureau Inc., 1974). Figures expressed in millions.

TABLE 8

PER CAPITA UNITED STATES MILITARY AND ECONOMIC ASSISTANCE TO LATIN AMERICA, 1962-1974*
(Gross Aid in Millions of Dollars)

	Economic Aid	Per Capita Econ. Aid	Rank	Mil. Aid	Per Capita Mil. Aid	Rank	Total Aid	Per Capita Total Aid	Rank
Argentina	186.1	$ 7.36	18	194.3	$ 7.67	5	380.4	$ 15.04	17
Bolivia	446.2	89.24	3	42.5	8.50	4	488.7	97.74	3
Brazil	2,197.0	21.69	15	312.0	3.08	15	2,509.4	24.74	15
Chile	799.0	76.83	5	152.6	14.67	1	951.6	91.50	4
Colombia	1,256.8	53.63	7	101.7	4.29	13	1,424.7	60.10	7
Costa Rica	146.4	73.20	6	1.7	.85	17	148.1	74.05	6
Cuba	-0-	-0-	20	-0-	-0-	20	-0-	-0-	20
Dominican Rep.	508.9	106.02	2	27.2	5.67	9	536.1	111.69	2
Ecuador	251.8	37.58	12	36.4	5.43	10.5	288.2	43.01	11
El Salvador	145.1	38.18	11	8.8	2.32	16	153.9	40.5	12
Guatemala	176.3	31.48	13	30.4	5.43	10.5	206.7	36.91	13
Haiti	64.2	11.46	17	0.7	.13	19	64.9	11.59	18
Honduras	130.2	43.40	9	9.7	3.23	14	139.9	46.63	10
Mexico	151.4	2.69	19	10.5	.19	18	161.9	2.88	19
Nicaragua	171.8	78.09	4	16.0	7.27	6	187.8	85.36	5
Panama	268.0	168.06	1	6.9	4.31	12	274.9	171.81	1
Paraguay	112.2	41.56	10	17.9	6.63	7	130.1	48.19	9
Peru	346.4	23.25	14	94.9	6.37	8	441.3	29.62	14
Uruguay	146.7	48.90	8	40.1	13.37	2	163.1	54.37	8
Venezuela	182.5	15.33	16	110.0	9.24	3	292.5	24.58	16

*Sources: *U.S. Overseas Loans and Grants* (Obligations and Authorizations July 1, 1945 to June 30, 1975) (Washington, D.C.: Agency for International Development, 1976), published once a year in May.

1973 World Population Data Sheet (Washington, D.C.: Population Reference Bureau Inc., 1974).

TABLE 9

THE RELATIONSHIP BETWEEN POWER, DEMOCRACY AND U.S. ASSISTANCE TO LATIN AMERICA
(Rho Values)

	Total Assistance $ Value	Total Assistance Per Capita	Military Assistance $ Value	Military Assistance Per Capita	Economic Assistance $ Value	Economic Assistance Per Capita
Political Democracy 1975	.14	-.04	.09	-.05	.11	-.05
Political Democracy Ave. 1965, 70, 75	.35	.11	.35	.22	.31	.08
System Stability	-.33	.16	-.31	-.21	-.23	.18
Concentration of Power 1975	-.04	.12	.02	.16	-.01	.12
Military Power Rating	.44	.29	.43	.32	.46	.25
Foreign Interest Power Rating	.11	.18	-.36	-.04	.03	.58
Landed Oligarchy Power Rating	-.11	.11	-.13	.04	-.13	.36
Industrialist Power Rating	.54	-.02	.62	.20	.47	-.18
Church Power Rating	.25	.29	.21	.17	.28	.28
Urban Proletariat Power Rating	.18	-.32	.18	.00	.12	-.35
Campesinado Power Rating	.00	-.08	.00	-.16	.02	-.08
Anti-Government Insurance Power Rating	.41	.06	.47	.34	.30	.06

assistance and ranked higher on the democratic index. Indeed they ranked higher before aid was given in larger amounts. Thus the per capita aid figure pushed down the rho value for democracy and U.S. assistance when compared to the dollar amount. Even so, if one could reasonably assume that U.S. aid had an equal impact on all citizens of the countries receiving aid then the per capita figure would be more useful. However, such an assumption may not be reasonable. Aside from the fact that a "trickle-down effect" is not totally effective even under the best of circumstances (e.g., propping up the monetary system is more immediately important to those borrowing and lending large sums of money and to those purchasing imported goods than to peasants without a line of credit or even participating in the cash economy), military aid can be considered to be equally beneficial only to those who have a vested interest in the goals of the military itself.

None of the rho values for aid and political democracy in 1975 proved to be statistically significant, suggesting that the aid program of the Alliance for Progress did not, at least in the eyes of the panel of scholars, contribute to the development of democratic institutions. The relationship between aid and "averaged" democratic rating coefficients for the 1965-1975 period was statistically significant at the .05 level (at least total aid and military aid) although the precipitous decline in the overall democratic rating of Latin America during this period seriously challenges the assertion that U.S. assistance can be causally linked to the building of democratic institutions. Therefore the decline in the Democratic Rating Coefficients of some of the major aid recipients (e.g., Brazil, Bolivia, and Chile) would seem to suggest that the correlation existed as a result of antecedent conditions, thus producing what could best be described as a spurious relationship. Indeed the 1975 index strongly supports this.

The impact of U.S. assistance on the power of various political contenders in the several Latin American countries was mixed. Moderately strong positive relationships were found to exist between U.S. assistance and the image of the power of the military, industrialists, and anti-government insurgents. A weak negative association was found between U.S. assistance and the image of the power of the landed oligarchy. Given the ALPRO emphasis on industrialization, agrarian reform, and anti-communism, these findings are understandable. One might speculate that the positive relationship between U.S. assistance and the anti-government insurgents could have resulted from popular resentment of foreign domination or perhaps indirectly as a result of the increased strength of the military resulting from U.S. assistance being used by radical groups as a justification for insurgency and related adventures.

Certainly it is noteworthy that the power of mass contenders, i.e., *campesinos* and the urban proletariat, is not as strongly associated with U.S. assistance as was the power of elites, further supporting the contention that a trickle-down effect from the aid program did not occur. Revelations that major rip-offs of U.S. poor relief assistance occurred (like the Managua, Nicaragua, earthquake case of December, 1972) and that the funds were pocketed by government officials bolster the more broadly pessimistic picture conveyed by our data.

SUMMARY AND CONCLUSIONS

We have seen the development of a pattern of U.S. intervention including the initiation and aftermath of the Alliance for Progress in Latin America. Despite the State Department's declaration to the contrary in 1968, the ALPRO was not a glorious success. The economic gains claimed by the late 1968 report were based largely on reported increases in the Gross National Products which, as was pointed out, do not reflect the true distribution of wealth. Moreover, ALPRO assistance correlated highly with the power exercised by "foreign interests" in the various Latin American states. Coincidentally, CLASCO scholars, meeting at approximately the same time the State Department report surfaced, analyzed Latin America's social, economic, and political problems in terms of the hemisphere's dependency on the United States. The greater the U.S. involvement in hemispheric affairs, the reasoning goes, the greater will be Latin American dependence.

Political democracy has not prospered since the Alliance was established either. The decline in the scholarly image of political democracy was greatest between 1960 and 1965, the formative period of ALPRO. Moreover, there is little evidence to suggest that U.S. assistance, either economic or military, did much to help the cause of political democracy in the hemisphere.

In the final analysis, one inference to be drawn from the quinquennial studies, including the 1975 power index, seems to be that U.S. involvement in the hemisphere has been to the detriment of Latin America both politically and economically. What, then must be learned from such experience? Certainly the military component of U.S. aid does not promote the humanitarian and political freedoms expressed in the Alliance for Progress' noble objectives, in many cases the same goals championed by humanists like Christian Bay.[16] It obviously has not solved the desperate life circumstances of easily eighty percent of Latin America's some three hundred million inhabitants. Another Third World scholar, Christian Potholm, says we would err both as human beings and as social scientists if we did not pass judgment on the kinds of goals and system thrusts that are prevalent in countries that we, as comparative politics specialists, choose to study.[17] That militarism and much of the U.S. aid program in Latin America are a baneful freedom-defeating/alienation-producing package has been documented in this chapter. Historically Leslie Lipson's geopolitical analysis has treated the military part of the question for practically all recorded time.[18]

At question, then, is the North American policy of giving military and other aid to regimes that crush popular drives for political involvement, that prevent reform, perpetuate elite privilege, and that commit atrocities against their citizenry. But who is most at fault, he who gives the repressive aid or he who puts it to use against his own people? Latin Americans must share a great deal of the blame for the socioeconomic conditions that spawn the political alienation and violence which have continually rent their societies. One distinguished Latin American statesman, Alberto Lleras Camargo, has even ventured to say that Latin Americans deserve the sort of governments they have.[19] This does not make the regimes any more humane, nor is the individual who suffers likely to receive much consolation from the knowledge that his fall into maelstrom is partly of his own doing. But Alberto Lleras has a point, nevertheless. Why this is so is a secret of the Latin American psyche, a syndrome transplanted from the "old world" that may be similar to what Edward C. Banfield has described as "amoral familism" mixed with various cults of arrogance, intransigence, violence, and human sacrifice.[20]

Latin America, blessed with many of the scarce resources which North American industries need to thrive and cursed with a political abyss between suppressed masses and elite-dominated regimes, has been an inviting target for imperialism. But let it be clearly understood that the imperialists have broad elite-based invitations to come; not all was done in the esoteric style of Theodore Roosevelt. Some Latin Americans were duped by their leaders, and by the United States, into believing that the Alliance for Progress would bring about a new life, eradicate deprivation, and motivate constructive political involvement. The Alliance instead became an opiate that addicted its user. In the light of the evidence presented herein, we think it appropriate to disagree with a recent contention to the effect that not economic development, nor land tenure, nor income inequality, not even foreign aid, have any relationship with violence or repression in Latin America.[21] At least in the minds of our experts, some, if not all, the above variables do correlate with violence, oppression, and the range of authoritarian tactics that are used in Latin America to perpetuate dictatorial regimes at the cost of great human suffering and in violation of basic human rights.

FOOTNOTES - CHAPTER FIVE

1. Teotonio dos Santos, "Crisis de la Teoría del Desarollo," in *La Dependencia Político-Económica de América Latina*, ed. Helio Jaguaribe, Aldo Ferrer, Miguel S. Wionczek and dos Santos, 4th ed. (Mexico City: Siglo Veintiuno, 1973), p. 180.

2. U.S. Cong., Senate, Committee on Foreign Relations, *Alternatives to Bilateral Economic Aid* (Washington D.C.: Government Printing Office, June 18, 1973), pp. 47-48.

3. James W. Howe (and the staff of the Overseas Development Council), *The U.S. and the Developing World* (New York-Washington-London: Praeger, 1974), pp. 23-24.

4. C. Neale Ronning, *Intervention in Latin America* (New York: Knopf, 1970), pp. 25-32.

5. An excellent concise treatment of the evolution of U.S. policy in Latin America is found in Edward J. Williams, *The Political Themes of Inter-American Relations* (Belmont: Wadsworth, 1971).

6. Thomas Melville and Marjorie Melville, *Guatemala: The Politics of Land Ownership* (New York: Free Press, 1971), pp. 50-52.

7. Jerome Slater, *Intervention and Negotiation: The U.S. and the Dominican Revolution* (New York: Harper, 1970), p. 13.

8. Slater, *Intervention and Negotiation: . . .*, p. 17.

9. *Dominican Diary* (New York: Dell, 1965), p. 230. See also Tad Szulc and Edward J. Williams, *Political Themes,* for a well-balanced discussion of the Dominican affair.

10. John Gerassi, *The Great Fear in Latin America* (New York: Collier Books, 1965).

11. Gregorio Selser, *Alianza para el progreso: la mal nacida* (Buenos Aires: Iguazú, 1964), pp. 266-67.

12. Selser, *Alianza . . .*, p. 275. It should be noted that the idea of "turning the screws" became acute during World War II. In point of fact, many believe that the United States could not have carried out its part of the war (thus the Allies would presumably have lost to the Axis powers) without the raw materials it got from Latin America. This, of course, laid a basis for continued exploitation thereafter.

13. Simon G. Hanson, *Dollar Diplomacy Modern Style* (Washington D.C.: Inter-American Affairs Press, 1970), passim.

14. Hanson, *Dollar Diplomacy* . . ., p. 132.

15. Hanson, *Dollar Diplomacy* . . ., p. 17.

16. Essentially freedom from coercion and freedom of political speech. See *The Structure of Freedom* (New York: Atheneum, 1968), p. 374.

17. Christian P. Potholm, *Four African Political Systems* (Englewood Cliffs: Prentice-Hall, 1970), p. 27.

18. See *The Democratic Civilization* (New York: Oxford, 1964), p. 592.

19. Alberto Lleras Camargo, "La arcaica América Latina," *Visión,* (Mexico City), 9 de octubre de 1971, p. 25.

20. See Edward C. Banfield, *The Moral Basis of a Backward Society* (New York: The Free Press, 1958); also Octavio Paz, *El laberinto de la soledad* (México: Fondo de Cultura Económica, 1959); and also his *Posdata* (México: Siglo Veintiuno Editores, 1970).

21. See Ernest Duff and John McCamant, *Violence and Repression in Latin America* (New York: The Free Press, 1976), p. 92. The authors of this work claim it to be an exercise in "comparative history," but their data base is questionable if not apocryphal, and this must affect the conclusions drawn therefrom. They argue for example that as of 1975 Paraguay was the only highly repressive personalist dictatorship in Latin America, a contention the people of Bolivia, Brazil, Chile, Nicaragua, and Panama would surely dispute. Personalist dictatorship may be accomplished by a "junta" of persons or by a single "magistrate" acting on their behalf. Semantic niceties alone will not give U.S. foreign aid a clean bill of health insofar as Latin America is concerned.

CHAPTER SIX
CONCLUSIONS

The trajectory of this study has ranged from literary glimpses of political life to a loosely constructed model of political chaos and atrophy in which democracy is an ephemeral political concept, through a series of measurements of the scholarly image of the democratic or undemocratic political process in Latin America. In the first chapter we sought to make a case for the use of literary-based evidence as an approach to conceptualization within a culture-relative context that would, hopefully, minimize ethnocentric bias. We hoped to tie this approach to our later measurements which of course do contain elements of cultural bias. These were inherited from the original Fitzgibbon experiment of 1945. But this defect has been partially obviated by the revised emphasis given the surveys as contained in the recent articles by Johnson that were cited earlier. Moreover, comparative problems at the statistical level have been further controlled by the reinterpretation of the Fitzgibbon-Johnson data that was devised by Miles Williams and is published for the first time herein.

Our second chapter attempted to operationalize the literary evidence proposal and elaborated a model drawn from one culturally well anchored source, the writing of the Colombian novelist Gabriel García Márquez. This is directly relevant to the issue of democratic political development and/or atrophy in Latin America. In constructing this model we see the questionable value of traditional labels (e.g., *liberal, conservative,* even *democracy* itself) and dramatize the semantic difficulties of conceptualizing the chaos which is Latin American political life. This chapter also suggests what may be a glaring weakness in our overall survey method--i.e., the absence from our respondent panel of scholars specializing in Latin American literature of social protest. It occurs to us that establishing two panels might be fruitful, one drawn from the social sciences as has been the case in past Fitzgibbon-Johnson surveys and the other drawn from literature and the humanities generally. For if we are to tap literary works for evidence with which to reflect upon quantifiable attitudinal data, we might also profit from the responses of specialized literary analysts and learn something valuable about the perceptions of our colleagues in other disciplines at the same time.

That democracy can be an ephemeral phenomenon in Latin America should be abundantly clear from the foregoing. And there is also doubt as to whether it is a more reliable guarantor of political stability than more authoritarian forms of rule. One of the implications of our Chapter Three is that across the years the authoritarian tradition (as in Venezuela) may give way to the forces of political democracy and that just because a given country may once have been a dictatorship does not mean that it is perpetually doomed to that condition. Yet tyrannies like Stroessner's Paraguay and dynasties such as Somoza's Nicaragua do not augur well for radical change within the foreseeable future. But that is what many Venezuelans believed during the Pérez Jiménez dictatorship prior to 1957. And on the negative side we have seen how during the years of the Alliance for Progress most of Latin America lost its previous ostensibly democratic thrust, culminating in the tragic events of Chile and Uruguay during 1973. In those cases it seems clear that the loss of democracy in states which had been its traditional bastions has benefitted no one except perhaps the military and a handful of oligarchs.

In looking closely at the evidence assembled in Chapter Three we should underscore that variables such as standard of living, educational level, and social legislation may be positively correlated with political democracy in terms of our scholarly images. But these same three environmental variables exhibit almost no correlation with stability and predictability in the political system. It would seem that there is also support for this conclusion in the Macondo syndrome if taken as evidence. One could speculate further that a regime which, to cite only one variable, took genuine steps to elevate its national literacy (educational level), might get itself into unwelcome trouble. Literacy is a tool which can be used to articulate demands and to organize threats. Other variables which correlate with democracy will also likely be threatening to an authoritarian regime. Too much social justice, even alleviation of hunger as in the quote from Graham Greene in Chapter One, may potentially upset the stability of an authoritarian government. Chapter Three also reveals cases in which there has been a directly inverse relationship between social legislation in particular and the general image of political democracy.

Our fourth chapter treating the relationship between democracy and the power of various interest groups yielded no great surprises. Where the scholars perceived the urban proletariat and the peasantry to be relatively strong the status of democratic practices seemed also to be reinforced. Conversely, the power of foreign interests, the military, and the landed oligarchy tended to depress political democracy. The same was true of the Church *vis-à-vis* democracy which, of course, is not to overlook certain revolutionary Christian sectors which have departed from the Church tradition of support for elites. There was a positive correlation between the power of industrialists and democratic strength which seemed to suggest *not* that industrialism causes democracy to flourish, but that many conditions necessary for a flourishing industrialism may also favor democratic political development. Along with this it appears that the conditions favorable to maintenance of a strong landed oligarchy tend to depress the democratic growth potential of mass based groups--not really a surprising finding.

It is also worth noting that on the basis of the evidence in Chapter Four industrialists tend to enjoy better growth conditions in South America than in Central America or the Caribbean generally, hence greater power ratings for the industrial sectors in South America. We can argue that this may make political democracy more viable over the long run in South America as the cases of Uruguay and Chile seemed to demonstrate until 1973--setbacks from which they may yet recover. The power of foreign interest groups tends to depress democratic ratings in Central America, a tendency reinforced by the hegemony there of *latifundistas*. We also note a distinct pluralistic bias on the part of our respondent experts as seen in the way they interpreted the five select criteria for democracy *vis-à-vis* the democratic potential ratings for mass groups as opposed to elite groups. A concentration of power (images) in one group tends to usurp that of other groups. Often the military is the usurping group, a consideration with obvious implications for United States foreign assistance to the entire area.

Our analysis of the relationship between power, democracy, and the hemispheric picture of interventionism generated relatively few statistically significant correlations. But the fact that so many comparisons were not significant suggests that the aid given by the United States to Latin American nations did little good in terms of the Alliance for Progress' rhetoric about promoting democratic political development. Had the aid's impact been more prodemocratic one would have expected a measurable change in the composite and individual scholarly images of items and countries over the years 1960-1975, but such, generally speaking, was not the case. This reinforces the widespread skepticism in much literature about the real meaning of United States assistance-intervention in Latin America. By implication the Macondo dicta on foreign intervention are supported.

We feel it is important to study the scholarly image of political democracy in Latin America not just because it may give us an imperfect reflection of the political process in that cultural area but also because scholarly opinions may influence public policy formation in the United States and elsewhere. The results of the 1975 survey were reported in summary form by the Mexican newspaper *Excélsior* on April 7, 1976, by a journalist who opportunistically sought to show that his host country was one of the three most democratic nations in Latin America according to the 1975 Fitzgibbon-Johnson findings. Ironically that same journalist, Armando Vargas, was complaining bitterly to the *Washington Post* and the *New York Times* three months later about the fact that his once independent publication *Excélsior*, then one of the hemisphere's most distinguished Spanish dailies, had been taken over by a government-engineered coup. In the turmoil that ensued *Excélsior* was reduced to puppet status and the Mexican government showed its true ilk as anything but democratic, the Fitzgibbon-Johnson ratings notwithstanding. What apparently happened over the years was not that Mexico had increased its "democraticness" in the eyes of the experts but simply that many of the remaining nations had deteriorated leaving Mexico a "winner" by comparison and default.

The case of Mexico and *Excélsior* places in bold relief a consideration that should be stressed: perhaps democracy is not the most culturally well anchored concept for application to Latin American political life. What happened to *Excélsior* was likened by the *New York Times* to the totalitarian regimes of Lenin and Hitler, surely antidemocratic images. Yet, were it placed in its cultural perspective, some defenders of Mexico's "single party democracy" might defend the *Excélsior* episode on the basis of system survival. That newspaper had for a number of years exposed governmental corruption and poverty in Mexico in a manner that caused many politicians in high places to lose face. What is democratic to some may be libelous and seditious to others. It is just as in the observation by Christian Bay that was cited earlier; in the antidemocratic state opposition to the regime more easily is seen as treason and sedition than in the democratic state where criticism is considered a healthy part of the political rejuvenation process. Clearly, freedom of political speech and press without fear of reprisal is a key criterion in determining the "democraticness" of any state.

The aftermath of the *Excélsior* case is worth citing briefly as a way of dramatizing the importance of the free speech and press criterion. *Excélsior's* ousted editor and publisher Julio Scherer García was able to defy the Mexican government's official monopoly on the sale of newsprint and formed a new weekly review called *Proceso* which began publishing in November, 1976. In the face of highly adverse international publicity the government refrained from closing that publication, at least as of the moment of this writing. Two articles from *Proceso* throw light on the practical aspects of democracy in Mexico (and by implication in other Latin American countries) and reflect upon the difficulties we impose on our panel of experts in asking them to evaluate Latin American political democracy.

Proceso's January 15, 1977, issue featured an article titled the "Strangulation of the Political Conscience" which commented directly on the concept of democracy:

> We always celebrate that which does not exist in order to convince ourselves of that which is not. We declare that two deputies have won seats in the national lower chamber in order to convince ourselves that we have democratic elections. We pay homage to agrarian reform and to the peasants to remind them that they won the revolution, even though they will never achieve power. We promise justice because we are ashamed of the injustice in which we must live. . .we have democracy with a manager, the official party PRI, which wants us to think that we live in a democracy. . .but it is the PRI which "democratically" practices violence against the people and then pretends to denounce its own violations as part of the democratic political facade.

And later the same year on June 20 *Proceso* carried a feature story about government intervention in telephones and espionage against most of the opposition political groups including unions and some businessmen. The article cited names of those who had been expelled from various parties as agents of *Gobernación*, the principal source of Mexican intelligence operations, and cited evidence that even high members of the official party PRI were spied upon to determine who might be a potential enemy of the regime.

This of course underscores Christian Bay's dictum stated above. The regime becomes an all-encompassing machine, a dominant class, which dares not trust even its own members lest someone become an "enemy." All outsiders are potential enemies. Yet one must also concede that Mexico cannot be an absolute tyranny in the "gulag" fashion for if it were a publication like *Proceso* would never have been able to emerge without reprisals. We do not, of course, know if such freedom of the press will prevail in Mexico. What is clear is that the single party regime in Mexico does not have a total death grip on all sectors of its body politic. It is still possible to criticize in Mexico. Converting that criticism into progressive and honestly administered public policy is quite another matter. But the experts who look at Mexico at the end of the present quinquennium will have to weigh the fact that some press freedom did exist in certain countries like Mexico. At the moment of this writing, and using the freedom of speech criterion alone, Mexico looks relatively democratic when compared to Chile, Nicaragua, and Uruguay to name just three.

In short, Latin America boasts a range of democratic forms from the "people's democratic dictatorship" of Cuba to the "dynastic authoritarian democracy" of Somoza's Nicaragua to the relatively competitive political openness of Colombia, Costa Rica, and Venezuela. The twenty Latin American republics surveyed herein can be arrayed along a democracy continuum that is culture-relative, a caveat which we have stressed throughout. It would probably be inappropriate to include all states of the western hemisphere (especially Canada and the United States) in the continuum for comparative purposes. One could, perhaps, correctly array the component states of Canada and the U.S. along such a comparative continuum.

Finally, in considering the status of democracy in Latin America we may ultimately have to distinguish between *social* and *political* democracy. Social democracy can be understood to encompass a range of social welfare benefits and equitable wealth distribution provisions made possible by leaders who may have achieved power via political violence or usurpation, traditionally undemocratic procedures. The original Fitzgibbon Index of fifteen items was heavily loaded with concepts that we could classify as social democracy, e.g., social legislation, standard of living, etc. The select five items created in the 1975 survey isolate the freedom variables which would imply a more "pure" political democracy, excluding coups and other nonpopular means of acquiring power. The concept of *social democracy* therefore may be culturally more appropriate for application to Latin American political life. That in a sense was one message emanating from the loose model we tried to draw from the Macondo syndrome, that the form of society's political organization and public administration may be less important than the impact it has on the lives of the citizenry.